After the Welfare State

*Politicians Stole Your Future . . .
You Can Get It Back*

Edited by Tom G. Palmer
Students For Liberty & Atlas Network

JAMESON BOOKS, INC.
Ottawa, Illinois

AtlasNetwork.org   StudentsForLiberty.org

Published by Students For Liberty & Atlas Network / Jameson Books, Inc.

Essays reprinted with the permission of the authors.

Edited by Tom G. Palmer
Cover Design by Jon Meyers

The editor gratefully acknowledges the assistance in preparing this book, not only of the authors and copyright holders, but of the members of Students For Liberty, most especially Clark Ruper, Ankur Chawla, Jennifer Jones, Morgan Wang, Jose Nino, and Matt Needham, who deserve a great deal of credit for bringing the book to publication. Moreover, he acknowledges the assistance in writing the essay "Poverty, Morality, and Liberty" provided by Diogo Costa, whose insights helped to shape the thesis, and by Lech Wilkiewicz, who helped to track down a number of obscure items. Finally, he thanks Emmanuel Martin, Brad Lips, and Michael Bors for reading the manuscript with care and catching errors, and Dara Ekanger for her expert work as a professional copy editor.

For information and other requests please write:

Students For Liberty
PO Box 17321
Arlington, VA 22216

or

Atlas Economic Research Foundation
1201 L Street, NW
Washington, DC 20005
www.AtlasNetwork.org

or

Jameson Books, Inc.
722 Columbus Street
PO Box 738
Ottawa, IL 61350
815-434-7905 for orders at special quantity discounts

ISBN: 978-0-89803-171-3

Printed in the United States of America

15 14 13 12   5 4 3 2 1

Contents

Section IV: Poverty and the Welfare State

Introduction

By Tom G. Palmer

Young people today are being robbed. Of their rights. Of their freedom. Of their dignity. Of their futures. The culprits? My generation and our predecessors, who either created or failed to stop the world-straddling engine of theft, degradation, manipulation, and social control we call the welfare state.

The welfare state is responsible for two current crises: the financial crisis that has slowed down or even reversed growth and stalled economies around the world, and the debt crisis that is gripping Europe, the United States, and other countries. It has piled mountains of debt on the shoulders of the most vulnerable among us—children and young people—and has issued promises that are impossible to fulfill. The crisis of unfunded obligations is approaching. It won't be pretty.

The essays in this volume are hardly the last word on the subject of the past, present, and future of the welfare state. Quite the contrary. They are presented in the hope that they will stimulate more thought, more study, and more soul searching on the subject. Accordingly, some are presented in a more academic style and some are presented in a more journalistic style; they draw on various intellectual disciplines. It is hoped that they will offer something of value to every reader.

As welfare states begin to collapse, implode, or retreat it's worth asking why this is happening. What role has the welfare state played in causing major international crises? Where did the welfare state come from, how does it function, and what did it displace? Finally, what will follow the unsustainable systems of today? This short volume is intended to help readers grapple with those questions and more.

Some consider the welfare state as sacrosanct, beyond question and inherently good. "Intentions," and only intentions, are what matter for such people. Intentions are certainly important to evaluating human behavior, but in evaluating institutions, we should also look at evidence and then investigate the incentives that have led to particular consequences. Those who look only to intentions close their minds to evidence and hard questions. They reason that if one questions the welfare state, it must be because one has bad intentions, which makes those who question the welfare state bad people; one should not listen to bad people, because bad people only try to trick you; so it's best to close your ears and your mind to avoid being tricked by them.

But not all minds are closed. Those with open minds believe that we should investigate whether the incentives established by welfare states tend to turn citizens against each other and to promote a system of mutual plunder, rather than mutual solidarity; whether current welfare state systems are unsustainable; whether politicians have responded to incentives to promise—and citizens to demand—much more than can be delivered; whether, rather than being a complement to democratic liberalism, the welfare state originated as an anti-democratic form of manipulation and tends to undermine democratic liberalism, sometimes subtly and sometimes spectacularly; and whether what the welfare state destroyed was in fact more humane, more effective, and more sustainable than what it put in its place. History, economics, sociology, political science, and mathematics should be our tools to understand and evaluate welfare states, rather than emotional responses or conspiracy theories. This little book is for those who prefer to ask hard questions and to pursue them with open minds. It's time to ask the hard questions about what the welfare state has wrought, whether it is sustainable, and what should come *after the welfare state*.

Tom G. Palmer
Jerusalem

Section I

Mutual Plunder and
Unsustainable Promises

The Tragedy of the Welfare State

By Tom G. Palmer

Many approaches to the welfare state focus exclusively on the intentions of those who support it, or offer mere descriptions of current income transfer programs. This essay draws on the economics of common pool resources to examine the welfare state as a dynamic and evolving system, a "tragedy of the commons" that has created incentives for its own exhaustion.

The welfare state has something in common with fishing. If no one owns and is responsible for the fish in the lake, but one does own all the fish he or she can catch and pull out of the lake, everyone tries to catch the most fish. Each reasons that "if I don't catch the fish, someone else will." Each of us may know that catching lots of fish now means that the lake will be fished out, but so long as others can catch whatever I don't catch, none of us have an incentive to limit our fishing and let the fish population replenish itself.[1] Fish are caught faster than they can breed; the waters are fished out; and in the end everyone is worse off.

Environmentalists, economists, and political scientists call that the "tragedy of the commons." It's a serious problem and is at the root of a great many of the environmental crises facing the world today, from depleted ocean fisheries to air and water pollution and other problems. But it's not limited to environmental problems. The welfare state operates like a commons, too, and the tragedy is unfolding as you read this. In modern welfare states, everyone has an incentive to act like the irresponsible fishermen who fish out the lake, except that the resource we're plundering is each other. Each person seeks to get as much as he can from his neighbors, but at the same time his neighbors are trying to get as much as they can from him. The welfare state institutionalizes what the French economist Frédéric Bastiat called "reciprocal plunder."[2]

Because we can plunder each other, people reason, "if I don't get that government subsidy, someone else will," and each has an incentive to exploit the resource to exhaustion. They justify taking government funds on the grounds that they're "just getting back what they paid in taxes," even when some of them are getting a lot more than was ever taken from them. Everyone has an incentive to take. This tragedy has a dimension not present in the case of the depleted fisheries: because we're plundering each other, we not only spend resources to plunder our neighbors, but we also spend resources to avoid being plundered by those same neighbors, which makes us all worse off to that extent. Not only are we plundered, but we are increasingly being plundered beyond all sustainable levels. The result is exhaustion. It's where we're heading now with welfare states:

- Governments have promised so many benefits to so many constituencies, all at the expense of each other, that the systems are unsustainable, but none of the recipients want to give up their benefits. We might do so in exchange for lower taxes, but we don't even get that choice. Governments can borrow the money and put the taxes off until later, that is, until after the next election, when they'll promise even more, to be financed by more borrowing.

- The pensioner demands an increase in state pension payments and even argues that it's just payback for what was paid in. Those pensions are financed on a "PAYGO" ("Pay-As-You-Go") basis, meaning that the taxes taken from current workers are paid out to current recipients. Any surplus of taxes over expenditures is just "invested" in government bonds, that is, promises to pay out of future taxes. That's all the US government's "Social Security Trust Fund" is: a big "IOU" "nestled in the bottom drawer of an unremarkable government file cabinet."[3] There really is no "Trust Fund." It's a gigantic scam. Today's young people are being forced to pay for their grandparents' retirement, their parents' retirement, and—if they have any money left over—they will have to finance their own. State pension schemes are indistinguishable in their structure from classic "pyramid schemes," also known as "Ponzi schemes" or "Chain Letters," which require that the base of people paying in increases indefinitely; when it stops growing, the pyramid collapses. Governments can postpone the inevitable by printing money or by borrowing money, but it's just that, a postponement, and with each postponement, the situation becomes worse. You can hear the rumblings of collapse now.

- The farmer demands a subsidy for his crops, which comes at the expense of taxpaying autoworkers; automobile firms and autoworkers demand "protection" from more affordable imports, as well as bailouts for failed firms. The trade restrictions raise the prices of vehicles for farmers and the bailouts for automobile firms raise the taxes paid by farmers. Autoworkers are plundered for the benefit of farmers, and farmers are plundered for the benefit of autoworkers. The cycle of reciprocal plunder goes round and round, with the vast majority of "winners" being losers after the cycle is completed. (Some, of course, who specialize in manipulating the political system and negotiating what Ayn Rand called the "aristocracy of pull,"[4] win much more than they lose. Politically connected Wall Street firms such as Goldman Sachs, mega agricultural firms such as Archer Daniels Midland, and others have profited handsomely from the aristocracy of pull.)

- We are boxed by tax systems into medical "insurance" systems (in the US payments for private insurance are tied to wages, while wage taxes finance "Medicare," and in Europe they are tied to taxes and in some cases to private insurers); this "third-party financing" affects the choices available to us. Since such pre-paid "insurance" typically pays for routine care, as well as catastrophic events (like injuries from car accidents, being diagnosed with cancer, or falling sick), we have to ask for permission from the insurer, whether private or state, before we get treatment. More often than not "health insurance" is not really "insurance," although it's called that; it's pre-paid medical care, which creates incentives among consumers to overuse it, and incentives among insurance companies and governments to monitor consumers to determine whether we qualify for benefits. As consumers we can't exercise the same choices as customers that we exercise with respect to other important goods, so we are forced to act like supplicants, rather than customers, and increasingly medical care is rationed by administrators, rather than purchased by customers.

Benefits to particular identifiable groups are concentrated and costs are diffused over vast numbers of taxpayers and consumers, giving beneficiaries incentives to grab for more, while the plundered have little incentive to defend their interests. Each one thinks himself or herself lucky when he or she gets a benefit, but doesn't stop to think of the cost of the benefits to everyone else; when everyone acts that way, the costs become enormous. The poor suffer the worst, because a trickle of benefits may seem like a boon to them, when their very poverty is both perpetuated by the welfare state and deepened by the hidden transfers from the powerless to the powerful caused by protectionism, licensing, and other restrictions on labor market freedom, and all the other privileges and special deals the powerful, the educated, the articulate, and the empowered create for themselves at the expense of the weak, the uneducated, the voiceless, and the disempowered.

Immigrants are systematically demonized as "here to get our welfare benefits." Rather than welcoming people to come and produce wealth, subjects of welfare states act to protect "their welfare benefits" by excluding would-be immigrants and demonizing them as locusts and looters.[5] Meanwhile, political elites loudly proclaim that they are helping poor people abroad by using money taken from taxpayers to fund a parasitic international "aid industry," dumping huge quantities of the agricultural surpluses that have been generated by welfare state policies (to subsidize farmers by guaranteeing floor prices for their products), and handing over loot to autocratic governments: in short, by internationalizing the welfare state. The entire process has been a disaster; it has undermined democratic accountability in developing nations, because the political leaders know that it is the foreign aid masters whose concerns must be addressed, not those of local citizens and taxpayers; it has fueled warlordism and civil war; and it has destroyed indigenous productive institutions.[6]

While citizen is set against citizen and citizen against immigrant in a vast system of mutual plunder (and defense against plunder), bureaucracies extend their control and both create and nurture the political constituencies that sustain them.

But mutual plunder is not the only salient characteristic of the modern welfare state. It has created one crisis after another, each an unintended consequence of foolish policies adopted for political reasons by politicians who don't have to bear the consequences of their policies. Two are gripping the world as I write this.

The Financial Crisis and the Welfare State

The financial crisis emerged at the intersection of human motivations and bad incentives. Those incentives were created by foolish policies, all of them traceable to the philosophy that it's government's purpose to control our behavior, to take from Peter to give to Paul, and to usurp responsibility for our lives.[7] The seeds of the current crisis were planted in 1994 when the US administration announced a grandiose plan to raise homeownership rates in the US from 64 percent to 70 percent of the population, through the "National Partnership in Homeownership," a partnership between the federal government and banks, home builders, financiers, realtors, and others with a special interest. As Gretchen Morgenson and Joshua Rosner document in *Reckless Endangerment: How Outsized Ambition, Greed, and Corruption Led to Economic Armageddon*, "The partnership would achieve its goals by 'making homeownership more affordable, expanding creative financing, simplifying the home buying process, reducing transaction costs, changing conventional methods of design and building less expensive houses, among other means.' "[8] That extension to the welfare state seemed to sound so reasonable to many. Why should people not own their own homes just because they haven't saved for a down payment? Or don't have good credit records? Or don't have jobs?

Why not make homeownership "more affordable" through "creative financing"? Government agencies, such as the Federal Housing Administration, and "government-sponsored enterprises," such as the Federal National Mortgage Association ("Fannie Mae"), were directed to convert renters into owners by lowering down-payment rates, drastically lowering lending standards among banks, increasing the amounts of money going into the home market by buying and "securitizing" more mortgages, and a host of other measures. It was a bipartisan effort at social engineering. The Federal Housing Administration under the Bush administration offered loan guarantees on mortgages with zero percent down payment rates. As Alphonso Jackson, acting secretary of the Department of Housing and Urban Development, gushed in 2004, "Offering FHA mortgages with no down payment will unlock the door to homeownership for hundreds of thousands of American families, particularly minorities." He added, "We do not anticipate any costs to taxpayers."[9]

The US government deliberately and systematically undermined traditional banking standards and encouraged—in fact, demanded—increasingly risky lending. Risks that turned out well would generate private profits, and risks that turned out badly would fall on the taxpayers, for "a banker confronted with these new relaxed requirements could off-load any risky loans to the government-sponsored enterprises responsible for financing home mortgages for millions of Americans."[10] Private profits and socialized losses characterized the intersection of welfare statism and cronyism.

Home prices went up and up and up as more and more money was pumped into housing. It was like a party. Everyone was feeling richer, as the prices of their homes sky-rocketed. People took out "adjustable rate mortgages" to buy homes bigger than they were able to afford, because they expected to sell them before interest rates went up again. Credit was easy and Americans took out second mortgages to finance vacations and boat purchases. More and more houses were built in anticipation of ever-rising prices. The result was a housing bubble of enormous magnitude. People bought houses to "flip" them and sell them to the next buyers. Meanwhile, government financial regulators worldwide rated as low-risk what were in fact high-risk loans, including both government debt (bonds) and mortgage-backed securities.[11] German banks bought Greek government debt and banks in the US and all over the world bought mortgage-backed securities that they were led to believe were guaranteed by the US government.

The interventionist policies of the US government to make homeownership more affordable, expand "creative financing," and destroy sound banking practices were coupled with the arrogance of global government financial regulators who were sure that they knew the real magnitudes of the risks—and market participants risking their own funds did not. The result was that the global financial system was poisoned with risky loans, bad debts, and toxic assets, with disastrous results. Mortgage defaults rose as interest rates rose, and those "low-risk" mortgage-backed securities that institutions had been encouraged to buy turned out to be not so low risk, after all. Savings were wiped out, home owners found themselves unable to pay mortgages, financial institutions crashed and burned, and economic output fell. Numerous distortions of incentives caused by the entire system of intervention in both housing and financial markets are to blame, but without the policy of the American welfare state of "making housing more affordable" and "creative financing," the financial crisis would not have happened. The global financial train wreck was the outcome of one bad policy piled on another; it was a train wreck set in motion by the welfare state.[12]

The Debt Crisis and the Welfare State

While governments in the US and some European countries were frantically pumping up a gigantic housing bubble, the explosion of spending on welfare state programs for retirement pensions, medical care, and many other programs has plunged the governments of the world into a debt crisis. Much attention has been focused on the huge increase in government debt, and it has indeed been staggering. At the same time, those numbers are small when compared to the accumulated mountains of unfunded liabilities, that is, promises that have been made to citizens and on which they are relying, for which there is no corresponding financing. If a private firm were to mislead the public and its principals about the magnitude of its obligations, as governments systematically do, the officers of the firm would be imprisoned for fraud. Governments manage to exempt themselves from sound accounting practices and deliberately and systematically mislead the public about the obligations they are loading onto the shoulders of future taxpayers. Governments find it easy to promise today to pay money in the future. But the future is arriving very fast.

Economists Jagadeesh Gokhale and Kent Smetters calculated (rather conservatively) in 2006 that the total federal budgetary imbalance for the US government in 2012 would be about $80 *trillion*. The budgetary imbalance is defined as "the difference in present value between what the government is projected to spend under current law on all expenditure categories—entitlements, defense, roads, and everything else—and what it is projected to receive in taxes across all revenue accounts."[13] That was in 2006; Gokhale is currently updating the numbers, which he predicts will be higher. As Gokhale wrote, "Add the likely health-care cost increases associated with the new health-care law and this number is probably too optimistic, but we won't know until my project nears completion. For Europe, I estimate an overall imbalance of €53.1 trillion as of 2010. That is, 434 percent of the combined annual GDP of twenty-seven EU countries of €12.2 trillion. That is also an under-estimate because the projections are made only through 2050 (unlike the US projections, which stretch into perpetuity)."[14]

That means that those promises cannot be fulfilled and will not be fulfilled. Taxes would have to rise to astronomical levels to fund even a fraction of the current promises. Governments are far more likely not only to default on their acknowledged debts (bonds held by creditors), but to repudiate the promises made to citizens for pensions, health care, and other benefits. They have been lying to their citizens for years about their finances and the lies are made explicit when the promises are broken because they *cannot* be fulfilled, as we are seeing unfolding before our eyes in Greece. One way to repudiate their promises is to turn on the printing presses and pay them with piles of paper money, with more and more zeroes added to each note, which is to say, the currencies in which the promises are redeemed would be dramatically devalued. (Inflation is especially harmful as a means of dealing with debt, for it both distorts behavior and falls disproportionately on the poor and those unable to shield themselves from it.) The welfare states we know may be collapsing in slow motion in some countries, rapidly in others, but they are collapsing all the same and, as always, the burden will fall mostly on those lacking the political connections and the sophistication to avoid the consequences.

Many people indignantly respond to such facts by citing their intentions, in disregard of consequences. "Our aim is to help people; we did not deliberately aim to crash the world financial system by intervening into markets to make housing more affordable and lowering banking standards, nor did we intend to bankrupt our country!" they say. As the philosopher Daniel Shapiro quite aptly noted, "Institutions cannot be adequately characterized by their aims."[15] The best aims in the world, if combined with bad incentives via the wrong institutions, can generate terrible outcomes.[16] The intentions of advocates of the welfare state are irrelevant to the outcomes of their policies.[17] Most "political philosophy," as it is commonly practiced, is about comparing one intuition about right and wrong with another. That, frankly, is not very helpful to the task of creating institutions that work, that are sustainable, and that are just. For that we need much more than the mere comparison of intuitions; we need history, economics, sociology, and political science, not merely moral theory divorced from practice.

The Future Is Imperiled, but Not Lost

The welfare states of today are directly responsible for the two great economic crises that are gripping the world: the global financial crisis that has turned economic growth rates negative in many countries and wiped out trillions of dollars of asset valuation, and the debt crisis that has rocked Europe and threatens to bring down some of the world's most powerful governments, currencies, and financial systems. Even the best of intentions can generate terrible consequences when implemented through perverse incentives and institutions.

The story is not all doom and gloom, however. We can get out from under the welfare state and its crushing debts, humiliating bureaucracies, and reciprocal plunder. It won't be easy and it will mean summoning the courage to stand up to special interests and manipulative politicians. But it can be done and it must be done. Those who have demonstrated in the streets against "budget cuts" (usually merely cuts in the rates of increase in spending) are demonstrating against arithmetic. You can't keep adding negative numbers to negative numbers and get a positive sum; the numbers don't add up. We need demonstrations in the streets on behalf of reason, of fiscal responsibility, of cutting back the state, of freeing and empowering people to decide their own futures. We need a rolling back of the state's powers so that it is limited to protecting our rights, not attempting to take care of us. We need clear-eyed decision making about the capabilities of the state. We need an end to the welfare state.

How the Welfare State Sank the Italian Dream

By Piercamillo Falasca

Journalist and researcher Piercamillo Falasca tells the story of how sound policies launched Italy as an economic success story in the 1950s and 1960s, but welfare state policies initiated when the population was young, the economy was growing, and the future seemed far away have bankrupted the country. Falasca is vice president of the Italian classical liberal association Libertiamo.it and a fellow of the Italian think tank Istituto Bruno Leoni.

"The growth of your nation's economy, industry, and living standards in the postwar years has truly been phenomenal. A nation once literally in ruins, beset by heavy unemployment and inflation, has expanded its output and assets, stabilized its costs and currency, and created new jobs and new industries at a rate unmatched in the Western world."

—President John F. Kennedy

During official meetings friendly words of praise may be customary, but what US President John F. Kennedy said in 1963 at the dinner given in his honor by Italian President Antonio Segni in Rome was a statement of fact. From 1946 to 1962 the Italian economy grew at an average annual rate of 7.7 percent, a brilliant performance that continued almost until the end of the '60s (the average growth over the whole decade was 5 percent). The so-called *Miracolo Economico* turned Italy into a modern and dynamic society, boasting firms able to compete on a global scale in any sector, from washing machines and refrigerators to precision mechanical components, from the food sector to the film industry.

The period 1956 to 1965 saw remarkable industrial growth in Western Germany (70 percent in the decade), France (58 percent), and the United States (46 percent), but all were dwarfed by Italy's spectacular performance (102 percent). Major firms, such as the auto-maker Fiat; the typewriter, printer, and computer manufacturer Olivetti; and the energy companies Eni and Edison, among others, cooperated with an enormous mass of small firms, many managed by families, in accordance with the traditionally strong role of the family in Italian society. At least one-fifth of a population of fifty million moved from the poor, arid south to the rich, industrialized north, changing their way of life, buying cars and television sets, mastering standard Italian, enrolling their children in schools, saving money to buy houses and to help relatives still living in their old villages. After 1960, rapidly rising living standards, as well as growing business and job opportunities, brought about an end to the flows of Italians to the rest of Europe and the Americas, ending that Italian *diaspora* that had driven almost twenty million people to leave their homeland in less than a century.

What was the magic formula of the Italian economic boom? Many years later a senator for *Democrazia Cristiana* ("Christian Democrats," a leading Catholic center-right party), said in an interview: "We understood and immediately realized that we couldn't drive Italian society. The country was stronger than politics, and even more clever. Don't do anything was a better choice than many government measures." Who was the "we" Senator Piero Bassetti was talking about?

In the very first years after the Second World War, a group of liberal market-oriented economists and politicians attained key positions in government, swept away Fascist legislation, and instituted democratic politics and free-market reforms. A central figure was the anti-Fascist journalist and economist Luigi Einaudi, one of the most prominent Italian classical liberals, who returned to Italy and served after the war as Governor of the Central Bank, then Minister of Finance, and finally President of the Republic; he greatly influenced the economic policies implemented by Prime Minister Alcide De Gasperi (1945–1953) and, after De Gasperi's death, by his successor Giuseppe Pella, and others.

Some of those figures may not be well known outside of Italy, but they represented an extraordinary "exception" for European political culture. After twenty years of Mussolini's Fascist regime and the horrors of war, that group of classical liberals represented the only hope for the nation to emerge from its totalitarian past into democratic capitalist freedom. The context they operated in could be hardly considered an easy one. Italy was a poor country that had been devastated by Fascist collectivism and war; most of the population was both unemployed and uneducated; infrastructure was absent or very poor; a powerful Communist Party threatened to replace Fascist collectivism with Communist collectivism; and state-controlled companies dominated much of the economy.

Luigi Einaudi's influence was crucially important. A careful monetary policy curbed inflation for at least twenty years (in 1959 the *Financial Times* celebrated the *lira* as the most stable Western currency); free-trade agreements helped Italy to re-enter the international market; a fiscal reform (the *Vanoni Act*, named for the minister who designed it) cut tax rates and simplified the tax collection system. In an era dominated by Keynesian ideas and easy spending, Italian public expenditure remained relatively controlled: in 1960 public expenditure barely reached the level of 1937 (30 percent of GDP, with a significant share of fixed-capital investments), whereas in other European countries it had risen dramatically.

A few, such as the famous jurist Bruno Leoni, warned of dangers if the people did not remember what had caused their newfound prosperity. Rising prosperity seemed the perfect occasion for new government expenditures and interventions. As early as the 1950s the Italian government established *Cassa del Mezzogiorno* (similar to Roosevelt's Tennessee Valley Authority, but in poor southern Italy). In the 1960s Italian governments passed legislation aimed at redistributing wealth, expanding government control of the economy (e.g., the nationalization of electric supply), and establishing a stronger welfare state.

In relatively prosperous Italy, redistributionist movements gained broad popular support. In 1962, during important negotiations on job contracts for metal workers, unions asked for shorter hours, more vacation, and more power to organize union activities in factories. *Partito Socialista Italiano* joined the ruling coalition with the Christian Democrats and the first "center-left government" was formed. In 1963, a public housing program undertaken through the nationalization of land aroused strong opposition from entrepreneurs' associations and private owners (among them the Catholic Church), which convinced *Democrazia Cristiana* to abandon the idea, but such collectivist causes dominated the rest of the decade and the 1970s.

Several important public policies adopted in that period laid the foundations for Italy's current crisis. The first was a weakening of fiscal discipline, due to a 1966 Constitutional Court decision that loosely interpreted the constitutional balanced budget constraint; that suspension of constitutional limits allowed the Parliament to pass laws for which annual expenses were covered not by fiscal income (taxation), but by the issue of Treasury bonds. That decision tore a leak in the public budget that grew larger every year. Luigi Einaudi died in 1961 and all his calls for fiscal discipline were quickly forgotten. Until the early 1960s the "primary deficit," which is calculated by deducting interest payments from the total budget deficit, was almost zero; it rose quickly after the Court's decision and accelerated after 1972, when deficit spending became a systematic policy strategy. In 1975 the primary deficit had already reached a dangerous 7.8 percent of GDP.

The second was the introduction of a generous pension system in 1969 (the *Brodolini Act*). The previous contribution-based mechanism was replaced with a redistributive system, according to which retirees received pensions that were not determined by the total amount of compulsory savings collected during their working years, but merely by their previous wages. A "social pension" for every citizen was established, along with a seniority criterion for pensions, thus allowing workers to retire early and a lax approach was adopted to awarding disability pensions in southern Italy, which was considered a surrogate for more effective pro-growth policies. Few paid any attention to the issue of financial sustainability. After all, the voters of the future do not vote today.

The third was heavier regulation of labor markets through the adoption in 1970 of the so-called Workers' Statute, including Article 18, which stipulates that if a court finds unjust the dismissal of an employee of a firm that employs more than fifteen employees with long-term fixed contracts, then the employee has the right to be reinstated. The burden of proof rests entirely on the employer. By making it very costly to *dismiss* employees, the law at the same time made it very costly to *hire* employees, which both reduced workplace mobility and encouraged illegal work.

The fourth established, through successive acts between 1968 and 1978, a nationalized health care system that is almost fully financed by taxes, meaning that there is little incentive for consumers to economize on use of medical services.

Finally, in January 1970, the government imposed a compulsory rule for all employees in the engineering and metal sectors, which substantially regulated and limited working times.

The long-run negative effects of those and other policies were obscured in the short run by Italy's still strong growth and by the low average age of the population. Generous pensions and health care expenses for small numbers of retired people were paid by large numbers of young workers. Year after year those policies, along with ever-heavier regulation of the labor and services markets, reduced productivity, made the labor market more rigid, dramatically raised the costs of hiring, and promoted ever-greater public expenditures and the accumulation of state debt, which in turn absorbed an ever-greater share of private saving.

Over time an aging population reduced the ratio between the working population and the retired population, making pension and health care systems more demanding and less sustainable. During the 1960s and the 1970s all European countries enlarged their public expenditures, but Italy literally went out of control, losing its image from the 1950s as a fiscally responsible country. Public spending rose from 32.7 percent of GDP in 1970 to 56.3 percent in 1993, spurred on in part by a reckless policy of hiring more civil servants to make up for the lack of private jobs, especially in the south. (That lack of work was, of course, largely related to the extreme costs of hiring imposed on the private sector.) While public debt had been stable at an average 30 percent of GDP during the 1950s and 1960s, it reached the astonishing total of 121.8 percent in 1994.

Thus ended the Italian miracle. Average GDP growth rate was still 3.2 percent in the 1970s, but it fell to 2.2 percent in the 1980s. Thanks to systematic devaluation of the lira, Italian firms could maintain their international competitiveness for a while (Prime

Minister Bettino Craxi announced the country had overtaken British GDP in 1987), but high inflation and public debt were clearly jeopardizing the future.

Various attempts at reform were made in the 1990s, especially after the financial and political crisis of 1992–1993, when the country risked a sovereign default and the post-war political system was swept away by corruption charges. Some privatizations of state-owned industries helped to lower public debt to a slightly more viable level. Minor changes were made to the pension system and in 1997 the Italian parliament passed legislation to modernize labor laws, but the political obstacles to abolishing Article 18's provisions (regarding the right to reinstatement of laid-off employees) led to the establishment of a cumbersome two-tier market, including both hyper-regulated and rigid old-style contracts, as well as flexible new fixed-term contracts.

Those reforms provided some fuel to an exhausted engine and postponed for a while the reckoning. The run, however, was over.

Italy is still a rich country, but the Italian political system acts like an impoverished nobleman who finds himself unable to adapt to his new condition. The deepest consequence of Italy's welfare state and welfarist interventions in labor markets is not economic or political, but cultural. The culture of welfare-state addiction is what has made change so difficult even in recent years, when Italy is experiencing a new debt crisis.

Contemporary Italians don't seem willing to roll up their shirt sleeves, as their parents and grandparents did, to produce wealth in a free and competitive economy, to give up unaffordable welfare state benefits in exchange for greater freedom, income, and prosperity. Can Italy return to Einaudi's classical liberal lessons and restore economic growth and a promising future? As has often occurred over the centuries, what happens in Italy can set an example for the whole world. For better or for worse.

Greece as a Precautionary Tale of the Welfare State

By Aristides Hatzis

Few contemporary democracies offer tales of institutional failure as startling as that of Greece. Despite a turbulent political history in the twentieth century, the Greek economy gained ground during decades of actual wealth creation, until the country's main parties started to compete on the basis of welfare statism, based on populism and patronage. Law and economics scholar Aristides Hatzis shows how short-term pursuit of political advantage through statist policies generated corruption, indebtedness, and political collapse. Hatzis is professor of the philosophy of law and theory of institutions at the University of Athens and writes about the Greek crisis at GreekCrisis.net.

Modern Greece has become a symbol of economic and political bankruptcy, a natural experiment in institutional failure. It's not easy for a single country to serve as a textbook example of so many institutional deficiencies, rigidities, and distortions, yet the Greek government has managed it. The case of Greece is a precautionary tale for all others.

Greece used to be considered something of a success story. One could even argue that Greece was a major success story for several decades. Greece's average rate of growth for half a century (1929–1980) was 5.2 percent; during the same period Japan grew at only 4.9 percent.

These numbers are more impressive if you take into consideration that the political situation in Greece during these years was anything but normal. From 1929 to 1936 the political situation was anomalous with coups, heated political strife, short-lived dictatorships, and a struggle to assimilate more than 1.5 million refugees from Asia Minor (about one-third of Greece's population at the time). From 1936 to 1940 Greece had a rightist dictatorship with many similarities to the other European dictatorships of the time and during World War II (1940–1944) Greece was among the most devastated nations in terms of percentage of human casualties. Right after the end of the war a ferocious and devastating Civil War took place (in two stages: 1944 and 1946–1949) after an insurgency organized by the Communist Party. From 1949 to 1967 Greece offered a typical example of a paternalistic illiberal democracy, deficient in rule of law, and on April 21, 1967, a military junta took power and ruled Greece until July 1974, when Greece became a constitutional liberal democracy. The economy of Greece managed to grow despite wars, insurgencies, dictatorships, and a turbulent political life.

Seven years after embracing constitutional democracy the nine (then) members of the European Community (EC) accepted Greece as its tenth member (even before Spain and Portugal). Why? It was mostly a political decision but it was also based on decades of economic growth, despite all the setbacks and obstacles. When Greece entered the EC, the country's public debt stood at 28 percent of GDP; the budget deficit was less than 3 percent of GDP; and the unemployment rate was 2–3 percent.

But that was not the end of the story.

Greece became a member of the European Community on January 1, 1981. Ten months later (October 18, 1981) the socialist party of Andreas Papandreou (PASOK) came to power with a radical statist and populist agenda, which included exiting the European Community. Of course nobody was so stupid as to fulfill such a promise. Greece, with PASOK in power, stayed in the EC but managed to change Greece's political and economic climate in only a few years.

Today's crisis in Greece is mainly the result of PASOK's shortsighted policies, in two important respects:

(a) PASOK's economic policies were catastrophic; they created a deadly mix of a bloated and inefficient welfare state with stifling intervention and overregulation of the private sector.

(b) The political legacy of PASOK was even more devastating in the long-term, since its political success transformed Greece's conservative party ("New Democracy") into a poor photocopy of PASOK. From 1981 to 2009 both parties mainly offered welfare populism, cronyism, statism, nepotism, protectionism, and paternalism. And so they remain.

Today's result is the outcome of a disastrous competition between the parties to offer patronage, welfare populism, and predatory statism to their constituencies.

What Is the Engine of Growth?

Wealth is created through voluntary cooperation and exchange. A voluntary exchange is not a zero-sum game in which gains are balanced by losses. It's a positive sum game which leads to the creation of additional value that is shared by the participants. (Involuntary transactions are often negative sum games, for in such cases the losses to losers are far greater than the gains to winners; a mugger may stab you in an alley and get 40 Euros from your wallet, but your medical bills and suffering will surely be far greater than 40 Euros, just as political struggles to redistribute wealth always involve expenditures of scarce resources on both sides—to despoil or to avoid being despoiled, and the total of those expenditures may well be far greater than the value of the wealth redistributed.)

Prosperity, whether called wealth, economic development, or growth, is positively related to the number of voluntary transactions that take place. The role of the government in this mechanism is to protect rights, on which voluntary exchanges are based, and to allow people to create wealth. The government can help this mechanism by securing property rights and enforcing contracts (thus making markets "regular," which is the original meaning of "regulation") and perhaps also by intervening carefully when there is a market failure, but without distorting the market and causing yet greater and more disastrous government failure.

Most contemporary governments have assumed another, more ambitious and dangerous, role. Not to "regulate" by establishing clear rules that make the market process "regular," but to intervene arbitrarily; not to help market transactions but to hinder them; not to protect positive-sum transactions that create wealth but to replace them with negative-sum transactions through subsidies and government spending. Most politicians today believe that if you just spend enough you will generate growth, and if there's no growth that means that they didn't spend as much as they should have. That road of accelerating government spending led to Greece's crisis, but it is not unique to Greece, for the same dynamic has led to the first credit downgrade in US history, and to today's European sovereign debt crisis.

Spending is popular for politicians because it buys votes in the short-term; after all, in the long-term we will all be dead, or at least not in power. It's popular with the voters because they tend to see government benefits as a windfall. They don't see the money as coming from their own pockets, but from "the government," or at least from someone else's pockets.

All the way back in 1974, Greek politicians forgot about economic realities. After the fall of the military dictatorship even the conservative government nationalized banks and corporations, subsidized firms, and increased the powers of the welfare state. Nonetheless, its policies were still limited in comparison with what the first socialist PASOK government did during the 1980s. After 1981, state intervention increased, and regulation and cronyism became the rule. That was also the policy of the governments up to 2009, with two minor exceptions: one of them was a short period in the early 1990s under reformist conservatives, during which almost all attempts at reform failed miserably, and the other, more successful, period was right before the entrance to the Eurozone in 2002 under reformist Socialists. But even then the numbers were fudged and the structural reforms were minimal.

How was so much spending possible, considering that Athens may well be the tax-evasion capital of the world? Since government revenue was limited due to colossal tax evasion and a perennially inefficient tax system, the rest of the money came from transfers from the European Union and, of course, from borrowing. As *New York Times* columnist Thomas Friedman aptly put it, "Greece, alas, after it joined the European Union in 1981, actually became just another Middle East petro-state—only instead of an oil well, it had Brussels, which steadily pumped out subsidies, aid, and Euros with low interest rates to Athens."

The borrowing became much easier and cheaper after Greece

adopted the Euro in 2002. After 2002, Greece enjoyed a long boom based on cheap and plentiful credit, because the bond markets no longer worried about high inflation or a devalued currency, which allowed it to finance large current-account deficits. That led to a crippling €350 billion public debt (half of it to foreign banks) but, more importantly, also to a negative effect that is rarely discussed:

> The transfers from the EU and the borrowed money went directly to finance consumption, not to saving, investment, infrastructure, modernization, or institutional development.

The Greek "party time" with the money of others lasted 30 years and—I must admit it—we really enjoyed it! Average per capita income reached $31,700 in 2008, the twenty-fifth highest in the world, higher than Italy and Spain, and 95 percent of the EU average. Private spending was 12 percent more than the European average, giving Greece the twenty-second highest human development and quality of life indices in the world. If you are impressed, remember that even those figures grossly underrepresented reality, because Greece's underground economy may amount to 25–30 percent of GDP!

The unreported income is mostly related to tax evasion. Even in 2010, some 40 percent of Greeks did not pay any tax and about 95 percent of tax returns were for less than €30,000 a year. Such widespread tax evasion cost the state budget an estimated €20–30 billion per year, i.e., at least two-thirds of the deficit for 2009.

Greece was morally and economically mired in corruption. Consider the tragicomic and infamous swimming pools of Athens. A swimming pool is an indication of wealth in Greece, so the Greek revenue service uses them to detect tax evasion. In 2009, only 364 persons declared that they had pools at home. Satellite photos revealed that there were, in fact, 16,974 private house pools in Athens. That means that only 2.1 percent of the people owning pools submitted truthful tax forms. The interesting question is not why the 97.9 percent lied, but why the 2.1 percent did *not* lie, since tax evasion in Greece is so widespread.

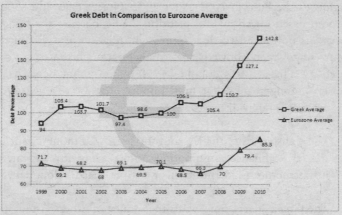

Greek Debt in Comparison to Eurozone Average

Source: Eurostat. See also: http://www.rooseveltmcf.com/files/documents/
BULLX-Greece-Aug-2011.pdf

Lying became a way of life in Greece. Still, one might argue that lying to protect what one has created is justified. But in Greece that wealth was not created, but simply borrowed. In 1980 public debt was 28 percent of GDP, but by 1990 it had reached 89 percent and in early 2010 it was more than 140 percent. The budget deficit went from less than 3 percent in 1980 to 15 percent in 2010. Government spending in 1980 was only 29 percent of GDP; thirty years later (2009) it had reached 53.1 percent. Those figures were hidden by the Greek government as late as 2010 when it admitted that it had not actually met the qualifying standard to join the Eurozone at all. The Greek government had even hired Wall Street firms, most notably Goldman Sachs, to help them fudge the numbers and deceive lenders.

That sorry state of the Greek economy was the result of two factors:

- the gross inefficiency and corruption of the Greek welfare state; and
- the thicket of impediments to voluntary economic transactions, created by welfarist interventions.

According to the annual *Doing Business* survey of the World Bank for 2012, Greece was one hundredth out of 183 countries around the world in terms of the overall ease of doing business. It was, of course, the worst place in both the European Union and the OECD (Organisation for Economic Co-operation and Development). Greece, a European Union member for the past thirty years, a member of the Eurozone for the past ten years, the twenty-fifth richest place on the planet, ranked below Columbia, Rwanda, Vietnam, Zambia, and Kazakhstan. As the *Wall Street Journal* put it: "a country has to work hard to do this poorly." Greek government policy was hostile to free enterprise and private property and severely obstructed labor and capital mobility, generally in the name of "social solidarity" and "fairness."

Greece Hates Business

Where Greece ranks, among 183 countries, on measures of doing business

Field	Ranking
*Ease of Doing Business	109
Starting a Business	140
Dealing with Construction Permits	50
Employing Workers	147
Registering Property	107
Getting Credit	87
Protecting Investors	154
Paying Taxes	76
Trading Across Borders	80
Enforcing Contracts	89
Closing a Business	43

*Overall ranking based on the 10 categories below

Source: World Bank, Doing Business 2010

Source: http://online.wsj.com/article/
SB10001424052748703961104575226651125226596.html

To start a new business in Greece in 2010 you needed an average of fifteen days and €1,101 when the average for the rest of the EU was eight days and only €417. Filing taxes took 224 hours a year in Greece; in the richest European Union state, Luxembourg, it took only fifty-nine. The ranking for the protection of investors was deplorable: 154th out of 183. Greece's best ranking was for the ease of closing a business; Greece ranked forty-third.

Almost all the professions in Greece are in some degree highly regulated and cartelized, which imposes costs on consumers and obstructs wealth creation. Add to that a hideously inefficient bureaucracy that costs Greece 7 percent of GDP, double the European average.

Interventionist bureaucracies tend to breed corruption. According to a Transparency International report, the cost of petty corruption was about €800 million ($1.08 billion) in 2009, an increase of €39 million over 2008.

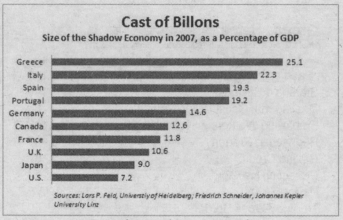

Cast of Billons

Size of the Shadow Economy in 2007, as a Percentage of GDP

Greece	25.1
Italy	22.3
Spain	19.3
Portugal	19.2
Germany	14.6
Canada	12.6
France	11.8
U.K.	10.6
Japan	9.0
U.S.	7.2

Sources: Lars P. Feld, University of Heidelberg; Friedrich Schneider, Johannes Kepler University Linz

Source: http://online.wsj.com/article/
SB10001424052748704182004575055473233674214.html

Unsurprisingly, Greece has the least competitive economy among the 27 EU members. According to the Global Competitive Index of the World Economic Forum for 2010–11, Greece ranked eighty-third, below countries such as Vietnam, Jordan, Iran, Kazakhstan, Namibia, Botswana and Rwanda. According to the 2011 World Investment Report by the United Nations Conference on Trade and Development, Greece is ranked 119th out of 141 countries in foreign direct investments. No wonder that over 50 percent of young Greeks are unemployed. That is the result of a business environment that discourages entrepreneurship, where bureaucratic costs are so high and there is so much corruption.

Greece's bloated welfare state has convinced many that their benefits have the status of "social rights." It would be political suicide for a politician or a political party to make significant cuts when the population has been accustomed to so many state-granted "rights" and an aging population has been promised huge health and retirement benefits.

Greece is the textbook example of the generation of unsustainable "rights." The government spends €10,600 per person on social benefits but brings in only €8,300 per person in revenues. This leaves a €2,300 deficit per person!

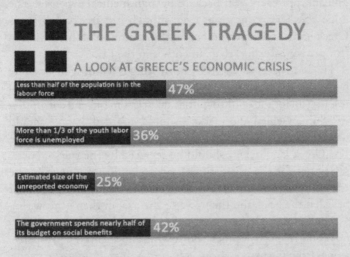

Source: http://fxtrade.oanda.com/analysis/infographics/
greece-economic-crisis

At the same time, wages in the public sector have risen in real terms (from 1996 to 2009) by 44 percent. (In some sectors they rose by up to 86 percent.) Employees received the equivalent of 14 salary payments a year, including two additional payments as bonuses (one for Christmas, half during the Easter vacation, and half before the summer vacations). Pensions also rose substantially.

A Greek man who had worked for 35 years in the public sector had the right to retire on a generous pension at the age of 58. Women could retire even earlier; if a woman had an underage child she could retire at 50. The average retirement age in Greece was 61; in Germany it was 67. Greece's over-65 population is projected to grow from 18 percent of the total population in 2005 to 25 percent in 2030.

One might argue that as expensive as the welfare state may be (it cost 19 percent of GDP in 1996, but 29 percent in 2009), at least it provides some sense of security and limits inequality. Not in Greece! Even though health and education are provided "free" by the state, the Greek family pays 45 percent of the total medical expenditure (mostly in bribing doctors, nurses, and public servants to do their jobs). Many (2.5 percent) Greek households go bankrupt every year because of high medical expenses. The same goes with education. Even though it's "free" at all levels, Greek households spend more for the education of their children (for private tutoring) than any other in the EU.

The long party financed by borrowing is winding down. The hangover is setting in. Now is the time to sober up, rather than reach again for the bottle of public debt. Cronyism and corruption should be tackled and markets should be freed. People should have the freedom to create wealth through voluntary exchange. The Greek kleptocracy should be replaced by the rule of law. A safety net for the misfortunate poor should no longer be the excuse for lavish benefits for the powerful and the wealthy that have left the poor and the powerless worse off than otherwise.

The lesson is that economic development and prosperity do not come from government borrowing and spending. Prosperity comes from the market, from voluntary transactions, from saving, investing, working, producing, creating, and trading. Government has an important job to do in creating the rule of law, the security, and the legal institutions that make those voluntary transactions possible; it neglects those important responsibilities when it creates instead giant bureaucracies, unsustainable entitlements, and a system of theft, corruption, privilege, and dishonesty.

Greece's predicament is severe. It will not be solved overnight. But it can be solved, with the right remedy.

Section II

The History of the Welfare
State and What It Displaced

Bismarck's Legacy

By Tom G. Palmer

To understand the functioning and the impact of the welfare state it helps to understand its origins, which are outlined in this chapter. This essay reveals the nature of the welfare state as a political system designed to sustain the power of those who crafted it. The welfare state is traced from the introduction of compulsory insurance schemes in imperial Germany to contemporary systems in Europe and America. Those welfare states shouldered aside pre-existing voluntary institutions. The institutions that were shoved aside by the welfare state provide us a vision of what is possible—societies of self-governing, self-respecting, independent, and prosperous people—without the welfare state.

Welfare states are distinguishable from socialist states. Socialism, as the term has been used for many decades, means at a minimum the attempt to plan the entire economy, known as "central planning," and more commonly it entails outright state ownership of the means of production; both entail the conscious attempt to use state planning to allocate capital and labor among competing uses. A socialist state will thus attempt to plan and direct the production of paper, vehicles, food, medicines, clothing, and other goods. Examples of attempts to create socialist states include the Soviet Union and its clients, Cuba, and the People's Republic of China before its partial turn toward allowing private ownership and markets. A welfare state, in contrast, need not entail state ownership of the means of production as a whole, although there may be significant state ownership in some industries, normally associated with certain services, such as education, medical care, recreation, and even housing, all of which are associated with "welfare."

A welfare state need not attempt to manage all productive activity, but it does undertake to be responsible for the welfare, or well-being, of the population. It is more extensive than a limited government that provides justice, defense against aggression, the rule of law, and perhaps a limited list of "public goods," as classical liberals propose. A classical liberal state limits itself to creating the peaceful conditions within which the people are free to secure their own well-being (welfare). Welfare states, in contrast, take responsibility for securing the welfare of the people, not only the conditions under which they seek their own well-being; accordingly, welfare states tend to dominate, or even to monopolize, provision of retirement security, medical care, education, and income security, and organize massive transfer payments, often justified in the name of transferring income from the "haves" to the "have nots," but typically shuffling—or churning—the great bulk of the transfer payments among the "haves."[18]

Welfare states do not transfer resources exclusively or even primarily to the poor. In many ways, welfare states victimize the poor for the benefit of those who are more capable of manipulating the system. (The same welfare states that deliver "food stamps" and other food subsidies to the poor also raise the price of the food they buy through agricultural subsidies, restrictions on less expensive imported food, and mandated minimum food prices, for example.) Welfare states achieve political stability by creating vast constituencies among all strata of society, from the wealthiest to the poorest. They are not primarily focused on "redistribution" of income downward, as a great deal of the redistribution of wealth goes in the opposite direction, from the poor to the rich. The great bulk of income redistribution in wealthier societies is churned among the middle classes, as money is taken out of one pocket and put into the other, minus the handling fees and inefficiencies generated by bureaucracies, political politicking, and cronyism.[19]

Origins of the Welfare State

The welfare state in its modern form originated in the late nineteenth century in Germany in the political maneuvering and "state building" of the German statesman Otto von Bismarck, the Iron Chancellor who defeated France and Austria militarily and unified the other German states into the "Second Reich" on the basis of "Iron and Blood."

Bismarck waged a lengthy political war on the free-trade classical liberals in Germany; they preferred peaceful means for the creation of a prosperous nation, as well as peace with Germany's neighbors, rather than war, colonization, and militarism. As a part of his state-building program in Central Europe, Bismarck pioneered the welfare state, which has since come to colonize much of the political space of the globe. Bismarck ushered in the German welfare state through a series of compulsory insurance schemes for accidents, health, disability, and old age, which he promoted and enacted in the 1880s. The militaristic Chancellor Bismarck called his measures "State Socialism," and stated in 1882 that "Many of the measures which we have adopted to the great blessing of the country are Socialistic, and the State will have to accustom itself to a little more Socialism yet."[20]

The historian A. J. P. Taylor explained that, "Bismarck wanted to make the workers feel more dependent on the state, and therefore on him."[21] It was, above all, a political stratagem to create a dependent population imbued with an ideology of national collectivism.

Bismarck confirmed that the purpose of his "State Socialism" was to generate the dependency, and thus loyalty, that a powerful Germany needed to dominate Europe:

> Whoever has a pension for his old age is far more content and far easier to handle than one who has no such prospect. Look at the difference between a private servant and a servant in the chancellery or at court; the latter will put up with much more, because he has a pension to look forward to.[22]

> I will consider it a great advantage when we have 700,000 small pensioners drawing their annuities from the state, especially if they belong to those classes who otherwise do not have so much to lose by an upheaval and erroneously believe they can actually gain much by it.[23]

Taylor concluded that "Social security has certainly made the masses less independent everywhere; yet even the most fanatic apostle of independence would hesitate to dismantle the system which Bismarck invented and which all other democratic countries have copied."[24] Indeed, the welfare state has made the masses "less independent everywhere," that is to say, more dependent everywhere. But we have now reached the point where we can, should, and must dare to dismantle "the system which Bismarck invented," for the welfare states of the world are fatally overextended.

It was the collapse in the 1930s of the over-extended welfare state of the Weimar Republic, widely known at the time as the most advanced welfare state in the world,[25] that ushered in dictatorship, war, and the most predatory and vicious welfare state the world has ever seen, the Third Reich. As the historian Götz Aly shows in *Hitler's Beneficiaries: Plunder, Racial War, and the Nazi Welfare State*, the National Socialist German Workers Party, also known as the Nazi Party,

> was propagating two age-old dreams of the German people: national and class unity. That was the key to the Nazis' popularity, from which they derived the power they needed to pursue their criminal aims. The ideal of the Volksstaat—a state of and for the people—was what we would now call a welfare state for Germans with the proper racial pedigree. In one of his central pronouncements, Hitler promised "the creation of a socially just state," a model society that would "continue to eradicate all [social] barriers."[26]

Aly goes on to say, "In a historically unprecedented fashion, they [the political leaders of the Third Reich] created the preconditions for the modern social welfare state."[27] The National Socialist welfare state, which instituted such an embracing system of patronage, dependence, and loyalty among the German population, was financed, as Aly documents in chilling detail, by means of stripping the Jews of their wealth (from their money, businesses, and homes down to their dental fillings, children's toys, and even their hair), confiscating the assets of enemies of the state, and looting the rest of Europe through requisitions and deliberate inflation of the currencies of occupied countries. It was also a pyramid scheme that required an ever-greater base of people paying into it to channel the loot upwards. Like all pyramid schemes, the Third Reich was doomed to fail.

The National Socialist welfare state was certainly the most destructive and vicious in world history, but it has closer connections to the less malignant welfare states we know today than many people realize. All welfare states begin by rejecting the classical liberal principles of limited government and individual freedom. They create systems of political control over the behavior of constituencies through deliberately induced dependence, typically justified through one doctrine or another of collective identity and collective purpose.

In the eighteenth and nineteenth centuries classical liberalism eliminated slavery and serfdom, liberated the Jews and other religious minorities from second-class status, fought for religious freedom, and liberated commerce, entrepreneurship, and creativity, resulting in the most astonishing increase in living standards for the masses in human history. Such changes engendered a cultural and political backlash against liberalism and a yearning for an imagined past of harmony and solidarity, in which "selfish" motives were subsumed by communal love; liberalism's success triggered reactionary responses. Friedrich Engels, later collaborator with Karl Marx in forging one of the most influential critiques of liberalism, condemned liberalism precisely for promoting peace and the achievement of the common good through freedom of trade:

> You have brought about the fraternization of the peoples—but the fraternity is the fraternity of thieves. You have reduced the number of wars—to earn all the bigger profits in peace, to intensify to the utmost the enmity between individuals, the ignominious war of competition! When have you done anything "out of pure humanity," from consciousness of the futility of the opposition between the general and the individual interest? When have you been moral without being interested, without harboring at the back of your mind immoral, egoistical motives?

> By dissolving nationalities, the liberal economic system had done its best to universalize enmity, to transform mankind into a horde of ravenous beasts (for what else are

competitors?) who devour one another just *because* each has identical interests with all the others.[28]

Moreover, Engels and others revived the old irrational hatred of charging interest on loans, an age-old resentment that combined anti-liberalism and anti-Semitism:

> The immorality of lending at interest, of receiving without working, merely for making a loan, though already implied in private property, is only too obvious, and has long ago been recognized for what it is by unprejudiced popular consciousness, which in such matters is usually right.[29]

The dynamism, the constant flux into which free markets placed economic and social relations, enraged elite critics who longed for stability, constancy, and moral certitude in economic relations:

> The perpetual fluctuation of prices, such as is created by the condition of competition completely deprives trade of its last vestige of morality. . . . Where is there any possibility remaining in this whirlpool of an exchange based on a moral foundation? In this continuous up-and-down, everyone *must* seek to hit upon the most favorable moment for purchase and sale; everyone must become a speculator—that is to say, must reap where he has not sown; must enrich himself at the expense of others, must calculate on the misfortune of others, or let chance win for him. . . . immorality's culminating point is the speculation on the Stock Exchange, where history, and with it mankind, is demoted to a means of gratifying the avarice of the calculating or gambling speculator.[30]

Anti-liberalism and anti-Semitism went hand in hand. In his essay "On the Jewish Question," Karl Marx attacks freedom of enterprise for Judaizing the whole of Christian Europe, for, in effect, dissolving earlier forms of solidarity and turning the Christians of Europe into his own caricature of Jews.[31] It was a theme that was to be repeated over and over in the next century.

As classical liberalism continued to extend more freedom to more and more people, the reactionary backlash against it grew, reaching full flower toward the end of the nineteenth century and the start of the twentieth in the anti-liberal doctrines of nationalism, imperialism, racism, and socialism. As Sheri Berman, herself a staunch defender of the welfare state (also known as "social democracy"), argues in her detailed history *The Primacy of Politics: Social Democracy and the Making of Europe's Twentieth Century*,

> The forward march of markets had caused immense unease in European societies. Critics bemoaned the glorification of self-interest and rampant individualism, the erosion of traditional values and communities, and the rise of social dislocation, atomization, and fragmentation that capitalism brought in its wake. As a result, the fin-de-siècle witnessed a surge in communitarian thought and nationalist movements that argued that only a revival of national communities could provide the sense of solidarity, belonging, and collective purpose that Europe's divided and disoriented societies so desperately needed.[32]

Marxist socialism was one political response, but while many intellectuals were attracted to it for its seemingly scientific claims about the inevitability of the replacement of capitalism by communism, others abandoned it when those claims did not materialize and turned to other means of direct action to attack and eliminate liberal individualism. Thus, as Berman notes,

> Although obviously differing in critical ways, fascism, national socialism, and social democracy had important similarities that have not been fully appreciated. They all embraced the primacy of politics and touted their desire to use political power to reshape society and the economy. They all appealed to communal solidarity and the collective good. They all built modern, mass political organizations and presented themselves as "people's parties." And they both adopted a middle ground with regard to capitalism—neither hoping

for its demise like Marxists nor worshipping it uncritically like many liberals, but seeking a "third way" based on the belief that the state could and should control markets without destroying them.[33]

The mass "people's parties" of Europe that paved the way for the welfare states of today have lost most of the exciting rhetoric that swept them to power. What has been left behind, however, are the unfunded liabilities attendant on grandiose promises of cradle-to-grave care, the debts and unfulfilled promises that pyramid schemes leave in their wake, and the social and economic turmoil of societies turned against themselves. (The elections of May 6, 2012, in Greece that were occasioned by the inability of that welfare state to fund itself brought to parliament the populist and extremist Coalition of the Radical Left Party and the openly fascist Golden Dawn Party, which should cause serious concern among supporters of liberal democracy who have any knowledge of twentieth century European history.)

The Welfare State Puts Down Roots in the US

In the United States, the welfare state arrived in a somewhat different form, although with strong similarities to the anti-liberal movements in Europe. Policies promoting "transfers" of resources, often through granting special privileges of various kinds, became entrenched after the Supreme Court case of *Munn v. Illinois* (1877), which allowed state legislatures to control the prices and rates of railroads, grain storage facilities, and other businesses, meaning that those same legislatures now had enormous power to benefit some interests at the expense of others. Chief Justice Morrison Waite wrote in the majority opinion:

> Property does become clothed in the public interest when used in a public manner to make it a public consequence, and affect the community at large.[34]

Thus began a new phase in what has come to be known as "rent-seeking," seeking one's own profit at the expense of others through means of political action. Farmers sought benefits at the expense of railroads; railroads sought benefits at the expense of competitors; manufacturers sought benefits at the expense of consumers; and on and on and on. During the so-called Progressive Era the transfer state bloomed on the American continent.

The economic collapse of the Great Depression followed the disastrous decisions of the Federal Reserve Board and the subsequent piling on of one bad policy after another, including the trade-destroying Smoot-Hawley Tariff, which set off a wave of protectionism that swept the world and led to a collapse of international trade. That experience led many to blame the severity and the duration of the Depression, not on destructively interventionist policies, but on *insufficiently* interventionist policies. During the 1932 presidential election Republican President Herbert Hoover boasted about how he had increased interventionism to deal with the consequences of previous interventions:

> Two courses were open to us. We might have done nothing. That would have been utter ruin. Instead, we met the situation with proposals to private business and to the Congress of the most gigantic program of economic defense and counterattack ever evolved in the history of the Republic. We put that program in action.[35]

Hoover promised more of the same interventionism if he were to be re-elected. Franklin Roosevelt campaigned for president against the strongly interventionist Hoover administration. Roosevelt both promised to abolish the disastrous policy of alcohol prohibition (which was probably as important as anything else in securing his election), and thundered against Hoover's overspending:

> I accuse the present Administration of being the greatest spending Administration in peace times in all our history. It is an administration that has piled bureau on bureau, commission on commission, and has failed to anticipate the dire needs and the reduced earning power of the people. Bureaus and bureaucrats, commissions and commissioners have been retained at the expense of the taxpayer.[36]

Despite campaigning against the interventionist policies of Hoover, the new Roosevelt administration quickly moved to adopt, continue, and adapt the policies of the Hoover administration into what became known as the New Deal, an incoherent series of interventions into economic processes that prolonged the Depression into the longest in American history.[37]

Much of that program, inherited from Hoover and extended by Roosevelt, included actions to keep prices from adjusting downward (which was the normal response to the Federal Reserve's huge reduction in the money supply); those measures included destroying vast amounts of food and creating a system of harmful agricultural subsidies that are still a mainstay of the American welfare state, creating massive public works projects, which delayed economic adjustment and prolonged the Depression, and establishing the "Social Security" system of compulsory retirement taxes, modeled on the German system that hid half of the tax on labor by calling it an "employer's contribution." The establishment of mass entitlement programs (often promoted in the name of "the poor," but in fact embracing increasing segments of the population until they become universal) is what characterizes the modern welfare state, and the similarities of the American system with the developments in Europe are striking, indeed.[38]

Many Americans do not know that they live in a welfare state, because they have been taught to identify the term "welfare" exclusively with government programs oriented toward transferring income to the poor, without realizing that everyone pays taxes for Social Security, Medicare, and many other gigantic (and broke) entitlement programs that trap them all in the welfare state. Moreover, although black Americans are a minority of recipients of "means-tested" welfare programs, most Americans associate welfare almost exclusively with poverty and black Americans, primarily due to the introduction of the counter-productive "War on Poverty" and the "Great Society" programs launched in the 1960s by the US government. The result was not quite what was promised, as the proliferation and expansion of programs targeted to the poor, and most significantly, to black Americans, resulted in social meltdown, the hollowing out of American cities, the withering of the voluntary organizations of civil society, the evisceration of the two-parent family, rising crime rates, and unprecedented levels of youth unemployment.

The sociologist Frances Fox Piven noted that the "War on Poverty" and the "Great Society" were rooted in the details of American partisan political struggle. In the 1950s, black voters were becoming increasingly important to the national electoral contest. Republican presidential candidate Dwight Eisenhower had received 21 percent of votes cast by black voters in 1952 and that percentage had risen to 39 percent in 1956. Richard Nixon received 32 percent of votes cast by black voters in 1960.[39] As Piven observed,

> By 1960 the Democrats felt that the black vote, especially in the cities, had become crucial in presidential elections. (The story of how Kennedy had captured Illinois by a mere 8,000 votes, the result of landslide majorities in the black South Side wards of Chicago, quickly became fixed in Democratic lore.) Yet blacks had not become integrated into urban political parties, nor were the agencies of city governments giving blacks a share of patronage, power, and services commensurate with their voting numbers. To remedy this imbalance, the Kennedy-Johnson administrations gradually evolved a two-pronged approach: First, they developed a series of novel programs directed to slums and ghettos, bypassing both state and local governments; second, they encouraged various tactics to pressure city agencies into giving more services to blacks.[40]

The key to the success of the strategy was to bypass levels of government that were dominated by groups who saw American black voters as threats to their patronage systems, notably state governments which, when run by Democrats, were often explicitly hostile to black voters (especially in the southern states then controlled by the Democratic Party), and northern urban governments, which were often run by coalitions of "white ethnic" (Polish, Italian, Slovak, etc.) Democrats, who were unwilling to share the spoils of patronage and political power with blacks. Thus, "The federal government had to take a unique initiative. It had to establish a direct relationship between the national government and the ghettos, a relationship in which both state and local governments were bypassed. . . . If the funds were channeled through local white ethnic political leaders, they would probably never reach the ghetto."[41]

Evidence for the strategic political nature of the "Great Society" was that the Republicans, when they took power, merely worked to shift the welfare benefits to their constituents. Sums of money that had been channeled directly into black neighborhoods were transformed into "block grants" to be administered by state governments (in most cases controlled either by white Democrats or by Republicans) and new forms of patronage were created to suit their political agendas, for, as Piven noted, such moves "are not being made because Republican policy is based on a clearer formulation of the nature of our domestic problems, as [Daniel Patrick] Moynihan and other critics would have it, but simply because Republican proposals are designed to deal with different political imperatives."[42]

The "antipoverty programs" of the American welfare state not only secured a major voting bloc for one party (and thereby polarized American partisan politics along racial lines immensely), but also had enormous consequences for the economic well-being of millions of people. As I write this, black youth unemployment rates are roughly double those of Asian and white youth and 50 percent higher than among Hispanic youth.[43] Black youth unemployment rates had been comparable to, and often less than, white youth unemployment until the Great Society programs were initiated, when the numbers began to diverge.[44] The poverty rate in the US, which had been falling steeply in the 1940s, 1950s, and even 1960s, stopped falling in the 1970s, when the Great Society programs were entrenched, and began to climb slightly, while labor force participation among young African American males dropped substantially.[45] Because of the visible failures of the "War on Poverty," many Americans, regardless of their race, associated "welfare" with programs targeted at inner city black populations. In fact, the money involved in programs targeted at the poor or at minorities comes to a fraction of the total controlled and allocated by the American welfare state.

Much of the money spent in the "War on Poverty" is, in any case, consumed by the bureaucracy itself. "With astonishing consistency," wrote Daniel Patrick Moynihan in 1973, "middle-class professionals—whatever their racial or ethnic backgrounds—when asked to devise ways of improving the condition of lower-class groups would come up with schemes of which the first effect would be to improve the condition of the middle-class professionals, and the second might or might not be that of improving the condition of the poor."[46] According to Richard A. Cloward and Frances Fox Piven, "The social-welfare bureaucracies were legislated in the name of the poor, but the poor were not their true clientele. The agencies were in fact oriented to other and far more powerful groups that could provide them with the legitimation and political support that public bureaucracies need for survival and expansion."[47]

The welfare state is not merely a collection of discrete and unconnected income transfer programs; it is a coherent *political strategy*, entailing harmful restrictions on the ability of the poor to improve their lot (to protect privileged groups from having to compete with them), coupled with income subsidies to partially compensate the poor for those grievous harms. The very politicians who portray themselves as friends of the poor when they distribute food subsidies to them, are the very same politicians who vote to keep food prices high by mandating floor prices for food; the same politicians who impose labor market entry restrictions through licensing and price unskilled workers out of the market through minimum wage laws offer income payments to those they forced out of employment through their policies. Walter Williams noted,

> The minimum wage law and other labor market restrictions do reduce employment opportunities and therefore the income of those forced out of the market. This fact suggests that, as a part of such union restrictive strategies, there must be a political strategy calling for various kinds of maintenance programs to provide income for those who are unemployed as a result of market closures: if the alternative to not working were starvation, it would present a socially volatile climate.

Thus it is very probable that labor unions will lead the support for income subsidy programs (e.g., food stamps, welfare, Job Corps, Public Service Employment projects, and various kinds of make-work programs) which represent a redistribution of income from society at large to those who have restricted the labor market in the first place. They *disguise* the true effects of market entry restrictions caused by unions and other economic agents by casting a few crumbs to those denied jobs in order to keep them quiet, thereby creating a permanent welfare class.[48]

The welfare state was, is, and will continue to be at base a political strategy to control people, not to produce greater well-being ("welfare") for them, but to manipulate them as political constituencies, in a new version of the ancient relationship of "patrons" and "clients." The manipulation is not only of the poorer elements of the population, but of everyone.

The political scientist Edward Tufte, in *Political Control of the Economy*, showed how transfer payments, mainly among the middle classes, are systematically manipulated according to the rhythm set by election schedules, in ways that reinforce "electoral-economic cycles," that is, electorally synchronized booms and busts, as governments time transfer payments to maximize disposable income just before elections, which tends to reinforce voter support for the ruling party.

The electoral-economic cycle breeds a lurching, stop-and-go economy the world over. Governments fool around with transfer payments, making an election-year prank out of the social security system and the payroll tax. There is a bias toward policies with immediate, highly visible benefits and deferred hidden costs—myopic policies for myopic voters. Special interests induce coalition-building politicians to impose small costs on the many to achieve large benefits for the few. The result is economic instability and inefficiency.[49]

The system of patronage and clientelism known as the welfare state has finally run up against something that ultimately can't be manipulated: *arithmetic*.

The total of government obligations, mainly for state pension, health, and other welfare state programs, has reached unsustainable levels. It's clearly evident on the streets of Athens, where crowds of "anti-government" rioters, composed almost entirely of government employees, have thrown petrol bombs onto other government employees, namely, the police. It's visible in the United States, where the last two administrations loaded on more debt than all previous governments in American history, not only to fund their global military presence and interventions, but even more to pay for uncapped liabilities in the forms of President Bush's "Medicare Prescription Drug, Improvement, and Modernization Act" and President Obama's "Patient Protection and Affordable Care Act" (also known as "Obamacare"). President Bush's folly alone added $17–$18 trillion to the budgetary imbalance.[50] The unfunded liabilities of President Obama's folly, if implemented, are harder to calculate, due to uncertainties about its implementation, but have been cautiously estimated at an additional $17 trillion over a seventy-five year time horizon, based on calculations and methods of the Office of the Actuary at the Centers of Medicare and Medicaid Services.[51] In 2008 Dallas Federal Reserve President Richard Fisher described "the math of Medicare," the US government's medical program, in stark terms:

> The program comes in three parts: Medicare Part A, which covers hospital stays; Medicare B, which covers doctor visits; and Medicare D, the drug benefit that went into effect just 29 months ago. The infinite-horizon present discounted value of the unfunded liability for Medicare A is $34.4 trillion. The unfunded liability of Medicare B is an additional $34 trillion. The shortfall for Medicare D adds another $17.2 trillion. The total? If you wanted to cover the unfunded liability of all three programs today, you would be stuck with an $85.6 trillion bill. That is more than six times as large

as the bill for Social Security. It is more than six times the annual output of the entire US economy.[52]

Those obligations will be repudiated because there is not enough wealth to pay them. They may be repudiated through inflation, which means that the burden would fall disproportionately on the poor and the disadvantaged and at the cost of distortions and dislocations in the economies of the world; or they may be repudiated by simply not paying them; or they may be repudiated by "tweaking the rules" to disqualify groups or categories from receiving promised benefits. The official debts of the world's welfare states are already at enormous levels, but the budgetary imbalances, when they are calculated to include total unfunded liabilities—the promises to provide benefits in the future, for which there is no revenue available—dwarf those officially acknowledged debts. Debts will not be paid and promises will not be fulfilled. Increasingly, people—and most especially young people—need to start thinking about alternatives to the welfare state.

Before the Welfare State . . . And After

Politicians love to point to what happened after they instituted a policy. "Look!" they tell us: "Since the introduction of our law against injuries, injuries went down!" thus taking all the credit for any improvements after the implementation of the new law. To test their claims, it's a good idea to look at the trend *before* the law was passed. If it was also trending down, perhaps at an even steeper angle, it undercuts the credibility of the claim that the new law was responsible for the improvements afterwards.[53] Trend line analysis is a useful way of checking whether policies have improved conditions. What was going on before the policy was implemented? Maybe something else accounts for the improvements.

Apologists for the welfare state want us to believe that before the welfare state, there was no provision for those in need, no medical care, no education, no provision for old age, "no welfare." That is not the case. In fact, in many cases the welfare state simply took over institutions and arrangements that had been created

48

by voluntary associations, and then proceeded to claim credit for them.

In the case of welfare institutions, prior to their displacement by the welfare state, there was a remarkable proliferation of voluntary institutions to help people to deal with the problems of life, from the need for medical care during times of misfortune to a friendly hand up when life had gotten one down. Historians have documented the remarkable story of the "friendly societies" that provided such "mutual aid" before the welfare state crushed them. Such societies provided social solidarity, insurance against misfortune, moral support, and much more, all on a voluntary basis. In the case of Britain, according to historian Simon Cordery,

> These collective-self-help organisations provided working people with the security of mutual insurance alongside opportunities for regular, ritual-based solidarity. They constituted the largest set of voluntary associations in Britain, reaching about six million members—equivalent to one-half of all adult males—by 1904.[54]

Too few people are aware that the friendly societies, which are documented in other chapters of this book, had more members than the far more extensively chronicled trade unions, far more support than the socialist movements that seized power in so many countries, and far superior systems of delivering social services and securing dignity for working people.[55]

Bismarck's State Socialist Imperial Germany used force to compel German workers to pay for "insurance," while more liberal Britain relied on voluntarism. As the historian E. P. Hennock observed,

> In Prussia, and subsequently the German Empire, insurance was compulsory for specified categories of the population. In England and Wales a Chief Registrar attempted rather unsuccessfully to monitor the action of a multitude of voluntary bodies. Yet in the 1870s voluntary insurance under the social and cultural conditions of England had penetrated the population more thoroughly than locally selective compulsion had

done in Prussia. By the early 1890s, after compulsion had been introduced across the [*German*] Empire, the voluntary system still penetrated English society at least as thoroughly. But once nationwide compulsion had been in force long enough to generate political confidence in its operation, its expansion accelerated and produced results well above anything achieved by voluntary means. The advantage of bureaucratically administered compulsion lay in procedures that, politically acceptable, could be progressively imposed on additional sections of the population.[56]

How valuable was any alleged increase in the velocity of extension of coverage when it meant replacing self-government among working people with bureaucratic governance that eliminated or drastically attenuated competition among service providers?

Moreover, as Hennock dryly notes elsewhere, the Imperial German system was established on an unsustainable "pay-as-you-go" basis from the beginning. Referring to the compulsory corporative system known as "Berufsgenossenschaften" (Occupational Associations) to which workers were assigned and which they were required to pay for their insurance, Hennock notes, Bismarck "discovered that fully inclusive *Berufsgenossenschaften* would not need to accumulate capital reserves to cover their future liabilities. Like regular state institutions they would be able to operate on a pay-as-you-go principle, meeting their obligations each year by raising the necessary contribution from their members in the year after. Since liabilities would accumulate only gradually, this arrangement reduced costs in the early years and made the proposed levels of compensation feasible after all. Although this would be achieved at the price of piling up problems in the future, it allowed any consideration of state subsidies to be put off for the moment."[57]

In other words, politicians found that they could kick the can down the road, because they did not have to deal with people who were free to make their own choices, informed by prices and other present indicators of future obligations and liabilities. Bismarck's State Socialism replaced responsible concern for the future with short-termism, with opportunism, through the pay-as-you-go system of deferring problems for future generations. It greatly weakened the voluntary associations that had been a mainstay of German society before them and when exported to Britain and other countries had the same effects there, as well. It was not the case that before the welfare state there was nothing. There was something better, but it was killed off by the state.

Similarly, voluntarily provided educational services had already spread literacy before the state crowded them out and started to reverse the trend. The historian of education E. G. West observed that "When the government made its debut in education in 1833 mainly in the role of a subsidizer it was as if it jumped into the saddle of a horse that was already galloping."[58] As educational scholar James Tooley has documented repeatedly, states presently claim almost universally to provide pupils with education, but frequently one searches in vain for the education allegedly being provided on a "free and compulsory" basis. Where the state solution of "free and compulsory" education is failing, voluntary provision is working, even for the poorest of the poor, as Tooley has documented in his studies and in his book *The Beautiful Tree: A Personal Journal into How the World's Poorest Are Educating Themselves*.[59]

The voluntary institutions of civil society that provided social services, medical care, and education were deliberately targeted for destruction in some cases, and were merely made redundant in others. Voluntary associations of working people who were engaged in solving their own problems were a major impediment to various statist parties and causes. "The great majority of us have a strong and confirmed belief in the voluntary principle as opposed to state compulsion," intoned a writer in a 1909 edition of the *Oddfellows' Magazine*.[60] The friendly societies of Germany and Britain were targeted for destruction precisely because they fostered independence, rather than collectivism, among the masses of the population. The voluntary associations of civil society atrophied in the US as the state asserted policies designed to create political constituencies and dependency. People everywhere became habituated to looking toward the state to solve their problems, rather than asking how they could work peacefully with others to improve their situations.

We can dismantle the welfare state and avoid the catastrophic effects of its collapse. If Greece is not a big enough warning, the fate of the Weimar Republic should concentrate our attention on the need to deal with the harm imposed on society by welfare states. We can avert catastrophe and we can replace the welfare state with institutions that are more just, more fair, more efficient, and more helpful to those who suffer in need.

The job of creating peaceful and orderly transitions from state-induced dependence, on the one hand, to freedom and independence, on the other; from perpetuated poverty to upward mobility; and from clientelism to active citizenship falls to the generation that is reaching adulthood today. Their elders have failed them. It is up to them to express in systematic and constructive involvement in public debate and policy formation their justified anger at the wastefulness, the irresponsibility, and the recklessness of their elders who thought that kicking the can down the road would make the problem disappear. We're down the road now, and this generation cannot kick the can any farther. It's the end of the road for the welfare state.

After the Welfare State

The welfare state is in crisis. The promises made in its name are a mixture of wishful thinking and outright lies. It emerged as a mechanism of power; it displaced, crowded out, and crushed voluntary and participatory institutions; it enervated and atomized societies and undercut personal responsibility; it substituted dependency and patronage for independence and rights. In usurping from citizens responsibility for their own welfare, it has turned them into clients, vassals, subjects, supplicants.

The ideology of the welfare state rests on a confusion between processes and outcomes. Welfare state advocates assert that they are aiming at noble outcomes, but pay little or no attention to the processes by which they are to be obtained. Even some self-professed liberals, who had worked to tear down the systems of power and subjugation that had oppressed men in the past, came to believe that beneficial outcomes could be legislated. Herbert Spencer called the emerging welfare-statist "social liberalism" of his day "the New Toryism," that is, the new conservatism, for they were adopting the methods of conservative, hierarchical systems of social control in the pursuit of what they thought of as liberal aims.

> The gaining of a popular good, being the external conspicuous trait common to Liberal measures in earlier days (then in each case gained by a relaxation of restraints), it has happened that popular good has come to be sought by Liberals, not as an end to be indirectly gained by relaxation of restraints, but as the end to be directly gained. And seeking to gain it directly, they have used methods intrinsically opposed to those originally used.[61]

Thus "social liberalism" came to diverge from authentic liberalism, now often known as "classical liberalism." The focus of reform became, not principles, rules, and institutions, but attempts to achieve outcomes directly through the use of coercive power. Outcomes are only very rarely subject to choice. Normally, we choose means (including rules and processes), not outcomes, in the hope that those means will yield the desired outcomes.[62] When policymakers forget that the means matter—in the case of human cooperation, that incentives matter, and that there are no magic wands to wave over the world to achieve outcomes directly, we can be sure that there will be terrible unintended consequences following on the policies they impose on us. The day is coming fast—and has arrived already in some countries—when the unintended consequences of welfare states have become unmistakable. It is time to end the magic show, to pull back the drapes and reveal that the wizards are just politicians and bureaucrats—normal human beings, like all the rest of us.

Those who believe in the moral worth, dignity, and rights of human beings should take their stand with the classical liberal Benjamin Constant:

> They [the holders of authority] are so ready to spare us all sort of troubles, except those of obeying and paying! They will say to us: what, in the end, is the aim of your efforts, the motive of your labours, the object of all your hopes? Is it not

happiness? Well, leave this happiness to us and we shall give it to you. No, Sirs, we must not leave it to them. No matter how touching such a tender commitment may be, let us ask the authorities to keep within their limits. Let them confine themselves to being just. We shall assume the responsibility of being happy for ourselves.[63]

The welfare states we have known are failing. It is time to prepare for what comes after them. If intellectual and political leaders insist on more and more state intervention to solve the problems of previous state intervention, our societies will slide further into cronyism, populist authoritarianism, and the bitterness of yet more broken promises. What is needed is more freedom, more choice, more responsible behavior, and more attention to avoiding the gross unfairness of loading future taxpayers with liabilities to provide benefits to present voters. Force is no substitute for liberty; neither does it produce security, nor happiness, nor prosperity, nor peace.

It is time to prepare for liberty, responsibility, and prosperity *after the welfare state*.

The Evolution of Mutual Aid

By David Green

Self-help and charity are not the only alternatives to the welfare state, as has often been asserted. Mutual aid, as instantiated by the friendly societies described by historian and political scientist David Green, provided solidarity, assistance, medical and other welfare benefits, and a framework for propagating moral values. David Green is founder and director of Civitas, an institute for the study of civil society based in London. He shows in his books how state provision of health insurance (initiated in Britain in 1911) and other elements of the welfare state undermined the friendly societies. Green is the author of numerous books, including Working Class Patients and the Medical Establishment *and* Reinventing Civil Society: The Rediscovery of Welfare Without Politics (*London: Civitas, 2000*), from which this chapter is extracted.*

Most histories of welfare provision tend to equate the improvement of welfare services with the growth of government involvement. Over the years the welfare state filled the gaps supposedly left by the market. More careful examination of the evidence, however, shows that the reality was very different. People in need because of their inability to earn enough to support themselves, whether temporarily or permanently, were supported in a rich variety of ways. Family and neighbors played their part but because their help was informal and undocumented historians have tended to underestimate it. Charity was also important and it is often supposed that organized welfare before the welfare state was left to charities, but by far the most important organized method by which people met the needs of their fellows was mutual aid. In Britain the friendly societies were the most important providers of social welfare during the nineteenth and early twentieth centuries.[64]

The friendly societies were self-governing mutual-benefit associations founded by manual workers to provide against hard times. They strongly distinguished their guiding philosophy from the philanthropy which lay at the heart of charitable work. The mutual benefit association was not run by one set of people with the intention of helping another separate group; it was an association of individuals pledged to help each other when the occasion arose. Any assistance was not a matter of largesse but of entitlement, earned by the regular contributions paid into the common fund by every member and justified by the obligation to do the same for other members if hardship came their way. They began as local clubs, holding their common fund in a wooden chest or strong-box, but the nineteenth century saw the gradual evolution of national federations with hundreds of thousands of members and carefully managed investments.

During the nineteenth century and until early in the twentieth century most families took pride in being self-supporting, but wages were such that if the breadwinner fell ill or died, hardship was the invariable result. The philosophy forged by this harsh reality was mutual aid. By the early years of the twentieth century the friendly societies had a long record of functioning as social and benevolent clubs as well as offering benefits such as: sick pay when the breadwinner was unable to bring home a wage due to illness, accident, or old age; medical care for both the member and his family; a death grant sufficient to provide a decent funeral; and financial and practical support for widows and orphans of deceased members. Medical services were usually provided by the lodge or branch doctor who was appointed by a vote of the members, but most large towns also had a medical institute, offering the services now provided by health centers. The societies also provided a network of support to enable members to travel in search of work.

Among the oldest was the Incorporation of Carters, founded in 1555 at Leith in Scotland, but it was not until the eighteenth century that the number of societies expanded rapidly.

Membership of the friendly societies grew steadily during the eighteenth century. By 1801 an authoritative study by Sir Frederic Eden estimated that there were about 7,200 societies with around 648,000 adult male members out of a total population of about nine million. This can be compared with a figure based on the Poor Law return for 1803 when it was estimated that there were

9,672 societies with 704,350 members in England and Wales alone.[65]

By the time the British Government came to introduce compulsory social insurance for twelve million persons under the 1911 National Insurance Act, at least nine million were already covered by registered and unregistered voluntary insurance associations, chiefly the friendly societies. In 1910, the last full year before the 1911 Act, there were 6.6 million members of registered friendly societies, quite apart from those not registered. The rate of growth of the friendly societies over the preceding thirty years had been accelerating.[66] In 1877, registered membership had been 2.75 million. Ten years later it was 3.6 million, increasing at an average of 85,000 a year. In 1897, membership had reached 4.8 million, having increased on average by 120,000 a year. By 1910 the figure had reached 6.6 million, having increased at an annual average rate since 1897 of 140,000.

It was at the height of their expansion that the state intervened and transformed the friendly societies by introducing compulsory national insurance.

Origins

At first the societies were local gatherings of men who knew each other and who met regularly to socialize, usually at a public house. All members paid a regular contribution which gave them an agreed entitlement to benefit. Some divided any surplus annually, often just before Christmas; others accumulated funds beyond a year. Some of the societies had no written rules; others had elaborate rulebooks. Each society was completely autonomous and it was this self-governing character which was always one of the strongest attractions to members. They were organizations which could be speedily adapted in any way to meet members' needs as and when they arose. When the government introduced a scheme for registration, very many societies preferred not to register, because to do so meant putting a legal limitation on their ability to adapt. As P. H. Gosden, the leading historian of the friendly societies, comments: "If a majority of the members wanted to spend part of their contributions on an annual feast they were not prepared to put themselves in the position where agents of the government might try to prevent them from doing so."[67]

Many early clubs were organized as dividing societies, that is each member paid an equal amount into the common fund and if there was a surplus after the payment of benefits at the end of the year, it was divided up equally among members. Such societies retained their popularity well into the twentieth century, but their disadvantages soon became apparent. First, the lack of an accumulated fund meant that they sometimes ran out of cash, and second, because of the annual renewal of membership very sick people were sometimes excluded at the year's end. These flaws led to the emergence of federations with accumulated reserves and a right to continued membership so long as contributions were paid.

Federations began to develop from early in the nineteenth century and became known as affiliated orders. By the time of the Royal Commission on the Friendly Societies of 1874 there were thirty-four of them with over 1,000 members each, with the Manchester Unity of Oddfellows and the Ancient Order of Foresters alone accounting for nearly a million members between them.

The emergence of federations had considerable implications for the internal government of the societies. The prevailing ethic in the earliest clubs was that everyone should have an equal say in common decisions. And since it was possible for all the members to meet in one place the normal practice was for decisions to be taken in a general assembly of all members. These early meetings were not only to reach decisions, but also for enjoyment, as the rules of the early clubs reflect. Invariably, they provided for the maintenance of order as well the distribution of beer to members.

The early institutions of manual workers tried out several different methods of self-government. First, there was the referendum: members who could not all meet in one place could still all vote. Second, there was the solution of having a governing branch, with power rotating from branch to branch. Third, there was the delegate meeting, each delegate being closely bound by the instructions of his constituents. Fourth was the representative assembly, comprising elected members free to take the decisions they believed best, in light of the facts of which they were aware and their constituents' wishes or interests as they saw them.

Gradually, a three-tier federal structure emerged—branch, district, and unity—which combined significant local autonomy with representation at district and unity (national) levels. In the affiliated orders, the branches—known as lodges among the Odd fellows and courts among the Foresters—retained wide powers, though final decision-making authority rested with an annual or biennial assembly.

The most important official was the Grand Secretary, sometimes with that title, at the other times variously called the Corresponding Secretary, Permanent Secretary, or High Court Scribe. The societies prided themselves on the absence of barriers to the advancement of any member to the senior office:

> the rights of every individual member are scrupulously respected and guarded; each individual has equal rights and privileges; merit alone is the medium through which posts of honour may be arrived at, and no artificial barriers are permitted to prevent virtue and talent from occupying their fitting station.[68]

It was only later in the nineteenth century that an intermediate level of organization was introduced between local branches and the national level. It was found advisable to spread the liability for death benefit more widely than amongst members of each branch, where even a few deaths in rapid succession could exhaust a small fund. Many societies evolved a district structure to spread the risk. Each district took its authority direct from the central body, but was governed by a committee of representatives from the individual branches. Apart from controlling the funeral funds, the districts also served as intermediate courts of appeal, and supervised the management of the various lodges, examining accounts and intervening where necessary. Lodges were required to send in yearly balance sheets and reports to the district as well as to the central body.[69] However, some branches disliked the additional control that the district system entailed and refused to affiliate.

By the mid-nineteenth century this process of evolution from the local club with its participatory democracy to the three-tier structure with a representative assembly and a full-time chief executive officer was well under way. But the original ideal of pure democracy retained much force and was often the yardstick against which proposed changes in the decision-making structure were judged. During the heyday of the autonomous local sick club it was generally held that everyone was equally well-equipped to hold office, a common belief in other working-class organizations, especially when new. For example, in a leading article in the *Clarion* published soon after the establishment of the Independent Labour Party in 1893, the editor (in the view of Sidney Webb the most influential member of that party) declared:

> It is tolerably certain that in so far as the ordinary duties of officials and delegates, such as committee men or members of Parliament, are concerned, an average citizen, if he is thoroughly honest, will be found quite clever enough to do all that is needful. . . . Let all officials be retired after one year's services, and fresh ones elected in their place.[70]

The friendly societies retained much of this spirit, and over many years structures evolved which balanced the need for competent performance of organizational duties and the desire for the maximum participation of members.

The Societies and Participatory Democracy
The friendly societies are of special interest because they sought to combine a high level of control by individual members with efficient administration. The welfare state is commonly criticized for excessive centralization, but this has not been a problem faced only by governments. Once the affiliated orders had ceased to be purely local clubs, the balance of power between the center and branches was a constant concern.

The affiliated societies produced a number of unique solutions to this age-old problem, solutions which minimized the costs and maximized the advantages for efficiency which a high level of participation can bring. The approach taken by the Foresters was that all lawful authority originated "with and from the Members at large." Power in the members, says the Foresters' first lecture, "is like the light of the Sun—native, original, inherent, and unlimited by anything human. Power in our Officers is only borrowed, delegated, and limited by the intention of the Members, whose it is, and to whom all officials are responsible." In the branch, all Foresters met on equal terms:

> In the Court, and before the law, no one is greater than another. All meet there on terms of perfect equality ... No office is too high for the poorest to aspire to; no duty too humble for the richest to stoop to. Intelligence to govern, ability to exercise authority with becoming humility, yet with the requisite firmness, and personal demeanor to ensure respect, are all the qualifications for office required; and these are in the power of every Member to acquire.[71]

The early clubs gave the branch chairman the power to impose fines for misconduct and the affiliated orders followed their example. The Foresters' Court Old Abbey, based in Guisborough, empowered its chief ranger to fine members 3d [three pence] for interrupting another or 6d [sixpence] for swearing or using abusive or insulting language.[72]

At the same time, the federations as well as the early clubs were keenly aware of the need to prevent presiding officers from abusing their power. Most societies impressed their expectations on a new chairman at his installation ceremony. The chief ranger in the Foresters took the following oath on assuming office:

> I, [name], having been elected Chief Ranger hereby solemnly promise and declare before you and the Brethren present, that I will do all within my power to promote the general welfare, peace, and harmony of the Court and that I will endeavor to act with impartiality in all matters connected with the office to which I have been appointed.[73]

The societies did not wholly rely upon moral appeals. Rules also laid down what a chairman could and could not do. The

General Laws of the Foresters, for example, stipulate that if the presiding officer vacated his chair "without permission of the assembled brethren, or without first providing some competent person to succeed him," or refused to put to the vote "any proposition that has been legally made," he could, if the offence was not "so flagrant as to cause a motion for his deposition," be fined five shillings for the first offense, ten shillings for the second, and up to twenty-one shillings for subsequent offenses.[74]

In a number of societies the lodge opening ceremony also served to inhibit the tendency for officeholders to become too powerful. In Manchester Unity, at the beginning of every meeting, each office holder was required solemnly to state the duties he owed to lodge members. The financial secretary, for example, had to say: "To keep a fair and impartial account between every member and the Lodge; to explain and balance such whenever required by you or a majority of the Lodge, and as far as in my power lies to keep the accounts clear and intelligible."[75]

In the early clubs the rotation of office was employed to ensure a sharing of the burdens and advantages of office, but gradually rotation gave way to regular elections. In the Manchester Unity, for example, with the exception of the financial secretary who held office at the pleasure of the lodge, it was customary for leading offices to change hands at each six-monthly or annual election.

Training Grounds for Democracy

Each friendly society had its peculiarities. But the affiliated orders share a tradition and are, for the most purposes, comparable. In the Manchester Unity the new member was eligible for any of the assistant offices: warden, guardian, conductor, and assistant secretary. The guardian's task was to guard the door and ensure that the correct password was given. The conductor helped new members through the initiation ceremony. The warden examined each person in attendance to establish their right to be present, and had custody of lodge regalia. Each lodge also had two secretaries, the elective secretary and the financial secretary. The main task of the elective secretary was to take the minutes of the meeting. Each of these positions, except that of financial secretary, was expected to change hands at every election.

In addition to the two secretaries, each lodge also had three major offices: the noble grand or chairman, the vice grand or vice-chairman and the immediate past noble grand. These offices changed hands regularly. All members were expected to seek to occupy these positions—to "go through the chairs" as it was called—and were required to prove themselves by holding the minor offices and by taking the degrees of the order.

But what was expected was not mere turn-taking. The holding of office was also a process by which the member could learn new skills. And for many manual workers the lodge offered opportunities for self-improvement lacking at the workplace. But the policy of changing the chairman every six months also carried with it the risk that the newcomer might be incompetent. To overcome this danger and to ensure that ready advice was available to the novice, each noble grand would appoint two supporters. They would sit on either side of him at meetings and whisper advice as the meeting proceeded. Traditionally, the noble grand chose an experienced right supporter, a member who had previously held the office and who was well informed about the rules and procedures. The left supporter was a friend whose task was to give unflinching moral support. In this fashion a high level of sharing of office was combined with efficient performance. And manual workers, whose role in the workplace was perhaps mundane and narrow, were able to develop their talents and share in the satisfaction of knowing that they were doing their bit to maintain the ideal of mutual service which inspired the friendly society movement.

A member who had held lodge offices could seek to hold still higher positions. An individual who had served in the four minor offices, taken the minor degrees, served as vice grand, noble grand, and immediate past noble grand, became eligible to sit for the past grand's degree or purple degree. If successful he became a member of the past grand's lodge and was eligible to hold office at the district and unity levels. The district officers were the district secretary, district grand master, district deputy grand master, and immediate past district grand master.

Above the district was the grand master, the deputy grand master, and the immediate past grand master. These positions were subject to annual elections. The board of directors comprised these three officers and nine other individuals elected by the annual conference. They retired annually but could stand for re-election. Each was required to hold the purple degree. The grand secretary was a full-time appointee, elected initially by the annual conference and holding office at its pleasure.

Respect for Rules and for Each Other
The leading societies invariably had an elaborate rulebook, which was almost an object of reverence to the manual workers who made up the membership. Before the rules every member was equal. Moreover, the rules were not externally imposed, they had been fashioned over the years by the members themselves: adopted, adapted, annulled, and revised regularly as circumstances changed. If the rules imposed constraints, as they must, they were constraints freely accepted by every member.

Friendly society members were proud of their rules. They were proud, not of the rules *per se*, but of the principles they embodied. The rules laid down what every member must contribute and what his rights were, and stipulated the duties of office holders. They limited the powers of office holders and ensured a sharing of the pleasures and burdens of office. And the rules maintained the autonomy of the branches from the district and unity levels within each federation. The societies were in a real sense ruled by laws rather than ruled by men, and to that extent they were admirable training grounds for participation in the democratic process of the nation.

Friendly Societies at the Turn of the Century
During the latter part of the nineteenth century new types of society began to develop as the conditions changed. When classifying the types of society it is customary to distinguish between societies which provided sickness benefit (general societies) and those which did not (specialized societies). The payment of sickness benefit was for most societies their biggest single task.

In 1910, before the 1911 National Insurance Act had made its impact, there were 26,877 societies of all types with 6,623,000 registered members.[76] The general societies are sub-divided as follows:

Membership of General Friendly Societies in 1910

	No. of branches or societies	Members
Orders and Branches	20,580	2,782,953
Unitary Accumulating	3,117	1,277,185
Dividing Societies	1,335	292,909
Deposit and Holloway	81	381,491
Total		4,734,538

Source: Beveridge, Voluntary Action, Table 21.

Total membership of special friendly societies in 1910 was 1,888,178, of which 855,962 were in death and burial societies; 403,190 in societies providing for shipwreck and miscellaneous losses; and 329,450 in societies providing medical care.[77]

Conclusion

Friendly societies, therefore, came in all shapes and sizes and it was this flexibility that formed an important part of their attraction. As Beveridge argued in *Voluntary Action*, it was remarkable how so many of the great institutions that proved popular began as a meeting of a dozen or so people in the evening after work, often in the back room of a public house. Some failed and some succeeded. In doing so, argued Beveridge, they changed the world:

In a totalitarian State or in a field already made into a State monopoly, those dissatisfied with the institutions that they find can seek a remedy only by seeking to change the Government of the country. In a free society and a free field they have a different remedy; discontented individuals with new ideas can make a new institution to meet their needs. The field is open to experiment and success or failure; succession is the midwife of invention.

Mutual Aid for Social Welfare:
The Case of American Fraternal Societies

By David Beito

Historian David Beito documents how Americans used their freedom of association to create a vast network of mutual-aid societies. With the possible exception of churches, fraternal societies were the leading providers of social welfare in the United States before the Great Depression. Their membership reached an estimated 30 percent of the adult male population and they were especially strong among immigrants and African Americans. Unlike the adversarial relationships engendered by governmental welfare programs and private charity, fraternal social welfare rested on a foundation of reciprocity between donor and recipient. By the 1920s, fraternal societies and other mutual-aid institutions had entered a period of decline from which they never recovered. The many possible reasons for this decline include the rise of the welfare state, restrictive state insurance regulation, and competition from private insurers. David Beito is professor of history at the University of Alabama in Tuscaloosa and the author of such books as From Mutual Aid to the Welfare State: Fraternal Societies and Social Services, 1890–1967; Taxpayers in Revolt: Tax Resistance during the Great Depression, *and with Linda Royster Beito,* Black Maverick: T. R. M. Howard's Fight for Civil Rights and Economic Power. *A longer version of this essay originally appeared in* Critical Review, *Vol. 4, No., 4 (1990), pp. 709–736.*

Of all the myriad examples that could be pointed to, including church, kin, and neighborhood support, the fraternal society stands out as one of the most fascinating, and most neglected, by welfare historians. Only churches rivaled fraternal societies as institutional providers of social welfare before the advent of the welfare state. In 1920, about eighteen million Americans belonged to fraternal societies, i.e., nearly 30 percent of all adults over age twenty.[78]

Fraternal societies were controlled by their members and organized around a decentralized system of lodges at the local level. Frequently, they included a secret ritual which was a collection of expressions, ceremonies, and other practices. Most members did not believe in the "magical" qualities of the ritual. Its main functions were to serve as entertainment and to test member solidarity. The lodge (with its raffles, bake sales, celebrations, and picnics) was also a center of community life in countless urban neighborhoods and small towns. Equally important, it furnished members and their families with an extensive system of mutual aid for social welfare.[79]

While the lines are often blurred, fraternal societies can be divided into two categories: the secret society and the fraternal insurance society. The chief difference between the two was one of emphasis rather than kind. Secret societies specialized in the *social* and *informal* components of mutual aid. The largest of them included the Masons, the Elks, and the Odd Fellows. The membership of the Masons alone constituted an amazing 12 percent of the adult male white population in 1930. Labor unions, by contrast, rarely included more than 10 percent of the labor force until the 1930s. Like most secret societies, the Masons eschewed written contracts or regularized guarantees of insurance for their members. "As a rule," Lynn Dumenil has written, "Masonic spokesmen were dismayed by the possibility that men joined Masonry for mercenary reasons, and they repeatedly emphasized that one of the Masonic pledges included the oath that the initiate had not been influenced by the desire for personal gain."[80]

Despite these official strictures, secret societies served as major conduits for mutual aid throughout American history. A Mason in good standing could rest assured that, if he so requested, the order would not only pay for his funeral but conduct an elaborate ceremony. If sick and in need, he could generally count on his lodge brothers to hang a collection hat on the altar or appoint a visiting committee. Masonic membership could open doors to employment and business advancement. Long-time Mason Samuel Gompers, better known as the president of the American Federation of Labor, related a particularly illustrative incident. In 1897, Gompers, while walking down the street, encountered a stranger, who also happened to be a lodge brother. After the two exchanged Masonic signs, the stranger admitted that he had been hired by a mining company to monitor the union leader. He then handed over negatives of pictures that he had taken of Gompers. Gompers recalled that he "frequently found that my affiliation to the Masonic order has been a protection to me."[81]

There was also a more visible side to the mutual-aid programs of secret societies. During the late nineteenth and early twentieth centuries, many of the larger orders embarked on programs to build orphanages and old-age homes for elderly members and their spouses. Thirty-nine jurisdictions of the Masons and forty-seven of the Odd Fellows had built homes for their elderly by 1929. In 1914, the average amount spent by the Masonic homes to care for each resident was more than $1,800. Although this was an era with no Social Security, few of the homes needed to be filled to capacity.[82]

Overall, the fraternal insurance society had a more substantial social-welfare impact than the secret society. The two shared the attributes of a lodge system of organization, rituals, and the rendering of informal mutual aid. The principal difference between them was that the fraternal insurance society offered its members formal insurance policies while the secret society did not. The keystone of fraternal insurance protection was the death benefit (actually a form of life insurance) paid to the beneficiary of deceased members. It was especially prevalent among wage earners. "Rich men insure in the big companies to create an estate," observed an article in *Everybody's Magazine* from 1910, "poor men insure in the fraternal orders to create bread and meat. It is an insurance against want, the poorhouse, charity and degradation."[83]

A large part of the mutual aid dispensed by fraternal insurance societies, much like that given by secret societies, was not a matter of record. Virtually all such organizations, regardless of their class or ethnic composition, repeatedly stressed the responsibility of individual members to provide aid to "brothers" and "sisters" in need. On this score, a spokesman for the Modern Woodmen of America (which called its members "neighbors" and its lodges "camps") wrote in 1934, "a few dollars given here, a small sum there to help a stricken member back on his feet or keep his protection in force during a crisis in his financial affairs; a sick Neighbor's wheat harvested, his grain hauled to market, his winter's fuel cut or a home built to replace one destroyed by a midnight fire—thus has fraternity been at work among a million members in 14,000 camps." Sociologist Peter Roberts described how fraternal societies among the coal workers of Pennsylvania at the turn of the century regularly sponsored raffles to help members who exceeded the time limit of their sick benefits.[84]

The most readily available guide to historical information (at least about the larger societies) is the records of the National Fraternal Congress (NFC), the major clearinghouse for fraternal insurance organizations. Societies affiliated with the Congress boasted over nine million members and 120,000 lodges in 1919. They paid an average death benefit of $1,100 (about $91 a month), roughly equivalent to average annual earnings for an American worker at the time.[85]

The smaller societies (many of them locally based and not members of the NFC) more often paid lower death benefits. To get a better picture of the average size of fraternal death-benefit policies overall, several local studies completed during the period need to be consulted. One of the best was a detailed survey of life-insurance ownership among wage-earning families in Chicago conducted in 1919 by the Illinois State Health Insurance Commission. The Commission found that 74.8 percent of the husbands carried life insurance, 58.8 percent of the wives, and 48.8 percent of the children under age 14. Just over half the policies carried by husbands were in fraternal orders. These policies averaged $768, which translates into a monthly average of over $64. Not accounted for in this figure were the many individuals who carried multiple life insurance policies in both private companies and fraternal societies.[86]

As a common feature, societies allowed elderly members to cash in the value of their insurance certificate either in a lump sum or in installments. Often, the beneficiary used the money to set up a small business. Despite this, it would be a misnomer to classify the fraternal death benefit as an old-age "pension" in the sense of a permanent retirement income. According to a study in 1930 by the New York Commission on Old-Age Security, the death benefit usually supplemented other means of support. The Commission estimated that about 43 percent of the elderly in the state were self-supporting through gainful employment, pensions, savings, or other forms of income, while family and friends supported another 50 percent (including housewives). Less than 4 percent of New York's aged depended on either public or private charity.[87]

What comparisons can be drawn between the fraternal death benefit and governmental poor relief? Probably the closest tax-funded analogue to fraternal death benefits were the mothers' pensions programs of the various states. Although restricted largely to widows, these were antecedents to the later federal Aid to Families with Dependent Children (AFDC). The number of beneficiaries served (as well as the size of benefits) was a far cry from that of fraternal societies. In 1931, 93,620 families (up from 45,825 in 1921) received aid from mothers' pensions programs, with each family getting a monthly grant of about $22. On the other hand, at least nine million (mostly working-class) individuals carried fraternal insurance that year. To say the least, Michael B. Katz's claim that "public funds have always relieved more people than private ones" looks highly dubious.[88]

Fraternal Health and Accident Insurance

During the nineteenth century, fraternal insurance protection centered on the death benefit. This always remained true, but by the early 1900s, many fraternal societies began to institute formal health and accident insurance as well. In 1917, an estimated 45 out of 59 fraternal orders in California offered a sickness or accident benefit, while 140 out of 159 in Illinois did so. These figures are less impressive than they seem, however. For one thing, the implementation of sickness insurance often was left to the discretion of local lodges. Equally important, even when a sick benefit fund existed, individual members frequently decided not to subscribe. If state and local studies are any guide, probably no more than 40 percent of fraternal members subscribed to a formal sickness benefit fund by 1920. Nevertheless, the percentage covered had increased rapidly in the previous two decades.[89]

Depending on the order and the particular lodge, the size, quality, and mix of fraternal medical benefits varied greatly. The typical medical benefit was a weekly cash payment. Fraternal society members in California were eligible for sick benefits ranging between $7 and $10 a week in 1917, while the maximum eligibility period averaged thirteen weeks. Because the average duration of illness for workers (in terms of working days lost) was less than two weeks, all but a small minority of beneficiaries had aid for the full period of need. Moreover, for those whose benefits had expired (only about 10 percent of those subscribing to fraternal health insurance ever applied in one year), it was a common practice in many societies to extend the eligibility time or pass the hat.[90]

Before the Depression, fraternal societies thoroughly dominated the health insurance market (at least among the working class), while their commercial competitors lagged far behind. In large part, the secret of fraternal success lay in the peculiar competitive strengths offered by the fraternal structure itself. Unlike private companies, fraternal societies were enviably positioned to check the threat of "moral hazard," the bane of the insurance industry. For health insurance, a major moral hazard is that individuals will take advantage of their insured status and overload the system with frivolous claims. The validity of a health insurance claim is highly subjective and thus difficult to verify. Life insurance has less daunting moral hazard pitfalls because beneficiaries can collect only if they present a death certificate. This partly explains why fraternal societies continued to dominate the sickness insurance market long after they had lost their competitive edge in life insurance.[91]

The fraternal society had several weapons in its arsenal to guard against moral hazard in sickness insurance claims. First, each new applicant for membership had to present a certificate of good health from a doctor. Second, and most importantly, fraternal societies, unlike private companies, could draw on extensive reserves of member solidarity. As the Social Insurance Commission of California noted, the "'mutual benefit' nature of the societies undoubtedly tends to counteract the tendency to malinger. Persons who might be unscrupulous in dealing with a commercial company are apt to be more careful when dealing with an organization whose financial condition is a matter of direct concern to themselves." The history of fraternal sickness insurance bears out economist Jennifer Roback's prediction that "moral hazard could be more effectively monitored within the group than outside it . . . . Put briefly, shirking can be more easily detected by people who share the same values and utility functions. The insurance group [or fraternal society] has a kind of social contract among themselves."[92]

By the second decade of the twentieth century, fraternal sickness benefits increasingly included treatment by a doctor. To name two examples, the Foresters of Reading, Pennsylvania, provided care by a doctor (including house calls) for $1 a year while, for $2, the Fraternal Order of Eagles covered everything except obstetrics and treatment for venereal disease. "Lodge practice" established an especially strong foothold in major urban areas. In the Lower East Side of New York City, 500 doctors had contracts with Jewish lodges alone.[93]

The favored method was for societies or individual lodges to enter into contracts with doctors to treat members and their families on a per capita basis. This method bore more than a faint resemblance to a modern health maintenance organization. It appealed in particular to younger doctors eager to establish a clientele or elderly doctors seeking a part-time practice. In later years, Samuel Silverberg, a lodge doctor during this period, recalled that the "society would pay me a certain amount for coverage for a certain number of patients—fifty cents for every single member every three months, seventy-five cents or a dollar for a family. Every member had a right to come to my office and ask me to call at his house. . . . The society member would recommend the doctor to his friends, and that way you could build up a practice. But it was hard, lots of running up and down tenement stairs."[94]

As lodge practice spread, it sparked opposition from leading doctors who feared that it would undermine their fee-for-service prerogatives. Typically, one leading physician, H. T. Partree, who, like Silverberg, had worked for a lodge early in his career, excoriated contract practice as "undignified competition." He bitterly recalled that:

medical service was rendered to the members at the rate of $1 *per capita* per year. I found that the number and variety of ailments requiring attention was something startling. The work was extremely unpleasant and my ire was deeply aroused at the thought that any lodge ... could be allowed for a single second to command medical service on such debasing terms.

The Shasta County Medical Society of California echoed the anti-competitive fears of the profession when it warned that lodge practice, if not limited in scope, would "place valuation on our services comparable to those of bootblack and peanut vendor."[95]

By the 1910s, medical societies and state commissions throughout the country went on the offensive to destroy the "lodge practice evil" or at least clip its wings. The House of Delegates of the California state medical society did its part by threatening to expel any doctor who contracted with an organization to provide care to families with monthly incomes in excess of $75. The Committee on Contract Work of the Erie County, New York, medical society recommended "antagonistic measures" against the contract practitioner "if persuasion fails to convince him of his error."[96]

Mutual Aid among Immigrants, African Americans, and Women

An impressive, but largely unsung, historical accomplishment of fraternal and other mutual-aid institutions was their role in the resettlement of the vast immigrant populations of the late nineteenth and early twentieth centuries. The foreign-born constituted 40 percent of the population of the twelve largest cities of the United States in 1900; an additional 20 percent were children of immigrants. Each immigrant group could turn to at least one aid society, and usually many more, to provide housing, English lessons, and information on employment.[97]

The immigrant fraternal society, a close relative of the immigrant aid society, contributed to remarkably high insurance rates among immigrant groups, including those from impoverished areas of Eastern and Southern Europe. By 1918, membership in the largest Czech organizations exceeded 150,000. A report by the Massachusetts Immigration Commission in 1914 identified two or more Greek societies in every town that had a Greek settlement. Springfield, Illinois, with a total Italian population of less than 3,000 in 1910, could claim a dozen Italian societies. Despite this rapid growth, the immigrant fraternal society had its detractors. Especially lukewarm were the Progressive reformers of the early twentieth century. Typically, Theodore Roosevelt declared that

> The American people should itself do these things for the immigrants. If we leave the immigrant to be helped by representatives of foreign governments, by foreign societies, by a press and institutions conducted in a foreign language and in the interest of foreign governments, and if we permit the immigrants to exist as alien groups, each group sundered from the rest of the citizens of the country, we shall store up for ourselves bitter trouble in the future.[98]

The popularity of the fraternal society among African Americans rivaled, and often exceeded, that among immigrants. Excluded from the leading white orders, African Americans founded their own parallel organizations. In 1910, sociologist Howard W. Odum estimated that in the South the "total membership of the negro societies, paying and non-paying, is nearly equal to the total church membership.... A single town having not more than five hundred colored inhabitants not infrequently has from fifteen to twenty subordinate lodges each representing a different order." Odum characterized fraternal societies as "a vital part" of African American "community life, often its center."[99]

The oldest and most famous African American society was the Prince Hall Masonic Order. William Muraskin estimates that during the 1920s and 1930s, the Order signed up over 30 percent of adult male African Americans in many small towns throughout the South. Local and state lodges provided a wide range of mutual-aid services, including medical insurance, orphanages, employment bureaus, and homes for the aged. The membership of the Prince Hall Masons reads almost like a "Who's Who" of African American history: Adam Clayton Powell Jr., Oscar

DePriest, Thurgood Marshall, Carl Stokes, Booker T. Washington, and W. E. B. Du Bois.[100]

The Masons represented just the tip of the iceberg of African American fraternal societies. African Americans organized parallel versions of the Odd Fellows, the Elks, and the Knights of Pythias. Many other societies, such as the True Reformers, the Knights and Daughters of Tabor, and the Grand United Order of Galilean Fishermen, did not have white namesakes. In 1904, the African American versions of the Prince Hall Masons, Knights of Pythias, and Odd Fellows had between them over 400,000 members and 8,000 lodges scattered throughout the United States. Five years earlier, W. E. B. Du Bois had estimated that at least 70 percent of the adult African Americans in the seventh ward of Philadelphia belonged either to fraternal societies or to less structured mutual benefit and petty insurance societies.[101]

Fraternal societies and other mutual-aid organizations gave African Americans from all classes access to insurance. Unlike their white counterparts, African American secret societies were more likely to offer formal life and sickness insurance as well as informal mutual aid. In 1919, the Illinois Health Insurance Commission estimated that 93.5 percent of the African American families in Chicago had at least one member with life insurance. African Americans were the most highly insured ethnic group in the city, followed by Bohemians (88.9 percent), Poles (88.4 percent), Irish (88.5 percent), and native whites (85.2 percent). The fact that African Americans worked overwhelmingly in low-paid and unskilled occupations, such as domestic service and menial labor, render these figures even more noteworthy. They also represent a striking testament to the resilience of African American families in an era of Jim Crow segregation and economic marginality.[102]

High African American insurance rates were not exceptional to Chicago. A 1919 survey of African American southern migrants in Philadelphia revealed that 98 percent of the families (regardless of income group) had one or more members insured, over 40 percent of them in fraternal societies. In the mining town of Homestead, Pennsylvania, in 1910, 91.3 percent of the African American families carried life insurance, slightly behind Slavs, at 93 percent, but ahead of native whites at 80 percent. Statistics of this sort so impressed Isaac Rubinow, a leading advocate of government old-age insurance, that in 1913, he singled out African Americans and immigrants as groups "where the habit of mutual insurance through voluntary association has developed to the highest degree in the United States."[103]

The fraternal lodge (despite its gender-specific connotations) was not an all-male preserve. The high participation of women in fraternal societies has not been given its due by historians. Many fraternal societies had women's auxiliaries, such as the Eastern Star for the Masons and the Rebekahs for the Odd Fellows. One of the largest of the fraternal societies managed and financed solely by women was the Ladies of the Maccabees. It called its lodges "hives" and offered members services that included maternity insurance. Fraternal orders touched women's lives in other ways as well. Most fraternal homes for the aged admitted the wives of members on the same terms as their husbands. While national statistics are not available, the Pennsylvania Commission on Old Age Pensions found that women constituted 76 percent of the residents of fraternal and benevolent homes for the aged in that state. Moreover, women were the major beneficiaries of death benefits.[104]

The Adequacy of Mutual Aid

How adequate was the mutual-aid protection offered by the fraternal society? To be properly addressed, the question needs to be approached on several levels. First, one might ask, adequate for what? The fraternal society catered to an abundance of individual needs: ethnic fellowship, entertainment, the establishment of business connections, as well as insurance and social welfare benefits. Not surprisingly, each society differed markedly in the goals it emphasized. The historian fond of uncovering the "one best way" is bound to be disappointed when studying the fraternal society. The Masons and the Odd Fellows stressed secrecy and solemn rituals, while the Knights of Maccabees and the Ancient Order of United Workmen concentrated on insurance protection. Still others, such as the Ancient Order of Hibernians and the Polish National Alliance, made ethnic solidarity a key credo.[105]

As a social welfare provider, the fraternal insurance society was not a panacea but, in the context of the time, it did a credible job of fulfilling the needs of members and their families. In the vast majority of cases, as we have seen, fraternal sick benefits covered the period of illness for which they were demanded. The same could be said for the utility of the death benefit. It helped cushion the financial blow after the loss of a family member (usually the chief wage earner).

For Americans of the 1990s, the "adequacy" of social welfare has taken on a cut-and-dried meaning. The question of adequacy has been reduced to the question of the amount of spending allocated. The conception of adequacy widely prevalent before the Great Depression, not only among fraternal societies, but among Americans in general, had connotations going beyond dollars and cents. It was closely tied to issues of character, self-respect, and independence. As the *Fraternal Monitor,* the chief voice of the fraternal movement, put it, "fraternalism is vitally concerned in matters having to do with self-help, individual liberty, and the maintenance of individual rights on the part of the people as a whole so long as such rights do not interfere with others." On numerous occasions, it predicted that an expanded governmental role in social welfare would discourage mutual aid and communal feeling. "The problem of State pensions," it charged, "strikes at the root of national life and character. It destroys the thought of individual responsibility."[106]

If measured by these less quantifiable standards of adequacy, the fraternal society equipped its members with advantages woefully absent in government welfare programs. In his study of social life in immigrant coal communities in 1904, Peter Roberts identified "independence, self-reliance, and foresight" as qualities fostered by the fraternal societies he observed. He added that

> the workingmen find pleasure in their lodges because the management of affairs is in their hands. . . . The results attained by employees in the management of their affairs may not be the highest, but they gain experience thereby and acquire business tact and an insight into the nature of the economic world which are of greater social value than financial considerations.[107]

Deserving and Undeserving Poor

It has become a rite of initiation for welfare historians to belittle the legitimacy of pre-Depression concerns about responsibility, character, and initiative in the provision of social welfare. Such ideas have been invariably dismissed as either instances of shopworn middle-class Victorian morality, or still worse, as part and parcel of an elite campaign to control the poor. For the same reason, historians have belittled the ancient distinction between "deserving" and "undeserving" poor as fallacious, and have praised efforts to make government aid to the poor an entitlement or a basic human right. In Katz's view, "the distinction between the worthy and unworthy poor has always been a convenient but destructive fiction" and has diverted attention from the more crucial social causes of poverty. Influenced by the views of Michael Walzer, Katz contends that categories of this sort cruelly stigmatize the poor as "objects of charity" and deprive them of their just due as equal members of the community. He has directed his heaviest fire against the "deserving/undeserving" differentiations of charity workers during the late nineteenth and early twentieth centuries.[108]

Katz and other welfare historians have been too hasty to dismiss the reasoning that underlay these charity-society dichotomies. To their credit, charity workers were willing to confront the complexities and subtleties of a thorny dilemma. Their distinctions among the poor, albeit imperfect, rested on a reasonable premise: that poverty, like other human conditions, has a multitude of causes and solutions. Along these lines, Mary Richmond, a prominent leader in the charity movement, observed in 1899:

> When we ask ourselves then, Who are the poor? we must answer that they include widely divergent types of character—the selfish and the unselfish, the noble and the mean, workers and parasites—and in going among them we must be prepared to meet human beings, differing often from ourselves, it may be in trivial and external things, but like ourselves in all else.[109]

The conventional welfare historians' diagnosis of poverty seems facile by comparison. If applied to public policy, the entitlement theory they champion translates into the simplistic (and misleading) credo that "there are no undeserving poor." Although it is not their intention, the net effect of this is to lump the poor together into an undifferentiated mass. Such an outlook is much more condescending to the poor than the approach of the charity societies. It is especially unfair to those working poor who, although eligible for welfare, refuse to apply because they take pride in remaining independent. By the logic of the entitlement theorists, these people are fools for trying to stand on their own feet.

Having said all this, the welfare historians do have a point. Private as well as government social workers during the late nineteenth and early twentieth centuries could go to condescending, intrusive, and paternalistic lengths to investigate the "worthiness" of recipients. The patronizing quality of case investigation techniques, such as "friendly visiting," was both unmistakable and disturbing.[110]

While Katz's critique of poor relief "categorization" as the uninformed product of "more fortunate" outsiders often fits charity and welfare bureaucracies, it loses its value as an explanatory tool when applied to the practices of fraternal societies. First, even those fraternal societies controlled by the poorest and most oppressed groups restricted aid to "deserving" members. One would be hard pressed to find a fraternal society of any economic class or ethnic group that distributed aid as an unconditional entitlement. The Georgia chapter of the Prince Hall Masons was typical when it forbade lodges to "receive or retain as a member . . . any man who is a common profane swearer, a reputed libertine, an excessive drinker, or one who is guilty of any crime involving moral turpitude or . . . any demoralizing practice."[111]

William Muraskin regards these fraternal-aid restrictions as attempts by oppressed groups to gain respectability by mimicking hegemonic Victorian, middle-class morality. This argument is not convincing. For example, how can it explain the popularity of similar restrictions in the mutual-aid programs administered by radical labor unions? The socialist and self-consciously working class Western Miners' Federation (a predecessor of the International Workers of the World) was typical in denying benefits to members when "the sickness or accident was caused by intemperance, imprudence or immoral conduct." Historians can, of course, take final refuge in claims that workers who supported these kinds of restrictions were victims of "false consciousness" or "mystification." But this is to say no more than that the historian holds to the ideal of a world in which each receives according to his need. This ideal offers no guidance to the realities of a world in which resources are limited and behavior often self-destructive.[112]

When viewed in this light, the whole enterprise of drawing analogies between charity/welfare aid eligibility restrictions and those of fraternal organizations becomes dubious at best. Charity-society admonitions struck a false note, not so much because of their specific content, but because they came from outsiders, most of whom had never been poor. Much like modern welfare-state bureaucrats, early twentieth-century charity workers could never truly understand the conditions of the poor nor entirely win their respect. It was not surprising that the poor resented and distrusted the impersonal and bureaucratic system which gave them alms.[113]

Charity and welfare aid restrictions revolved around an adversarial donor and recipient relationship, while those of fraternal societies rested on principles of reciprocity. At bottom, adversarial relationships between donor and receiver seem endemic to *any* impersonal poor relief system (public or private, entitlement-based or means-tested) controlled and funded by distant bureaucrats and other outsiders (including the taxpayer). Donor and recipient in the fraternal society were peers in the same organization. They often knew each other well on a personal level. While the process of deciding aid eligibility by fraternal societies certainly provoked its share of tension and oversimplification, it rarely had the degrading and patronizing quality of charity or welfare bureaucracies, since it was usually a matter of poor people classifying the aid worthiness or unworthiness of other poor people.

This fraternal idea of reciprocity, of course, entailed mutual obligations between members and the organization to which they belonged. It was wholly antagonistic to this idea that the donor should dole out benefits as a one-way entitlement to the recipient. To underline this point, Walter Basye, editor of the *Fraternal Monitor*, asserted that "fraternity, like religion or a savings bank, gives most to those who put in most. And the best deposit in the bank of fraternity is heart-felt interest and support."[114]

While fraternal society benefits were not unconditional entitlements, neither could they be properly classified as charity. Fraternal society leaders were just as critical of paternalistic charity as modern welfare historians. The manual of the Colored Knights of Pythias declared that the "sick among our brethren are not left to the cold hand of public charity; they are visited, and their wants provided for out of the funds they themselves have contributed to raise, and which, in time of need, they honorably claim without the humiliation of suing parochial or individual relief—from which the freeborn mind recoils with disdain." In 1910, a Mexican-American fraternal (*mutualista*) journal proudly proclaimed that "one will never see Mexican tramps, not even the most indigent, because he always works regardless of his age or his social and education conditions, to win his daily bread with dignity."[115]

The aid restrictions of fraternal societies rested on an ethic of solidarity. By limiting benefits to members deemed deserving of this solidarity, they shared common ground with labor unions. In labor unions, members who violated certain restrictions (by not paying dues or working during a strike, for example) lost their claim to benefits. The one major difference between labor and fraternal organizations was that the former could, and often did, use force to coerce recalcitrants while the latter had to depend entirely on voluntary compliance and moral sanctions.

Mutual Aid, Then and Now

The rich historical record of mutual aid and self-help poses a striking contrast to the present social and economic life of the very poor. When considering housing quality, income, and consumer goods, the population of the early twentieth-century slum would have good reason to envy the current "underclass." The envy would probably be on the other side, however, when it comes to the strength of community ties, family solidarity, independence, hope for the future, and safe streets. These and other measures are vital even if not easily quantifiable.[116]

Some of the most cogent descriptions of this transformation

have been penned by sociologist William Julius Wilson. Although Wilson rejects a return to the limited government role of the pre-welfare state era, he has repeatedly pointed to the palpable decline in the living conditions of those who must inhabit today's slums. "Blacks in Harlem and in other ghetto neighborhoods," he writes, "did not hesitate to sleep in parks, on fire escapes, and on rooftops during hot summer nights in the 1940s and 1950s, and whites frequently visited inner-city taverns and nightclubs. There was crime, to be sure, but it had not reached the point where people were fearful of walking the streets at night, despite the overwhelming poverty in the area."[117]

James Borchert also has noted the contrast between the past and present inner city. In *Alley Life in Washington*, he comments at length on the absence of what might be called today a psychology of dependence among African American and white slum dwellers in Washington, DC, during the early twentieth century. As Borchert puts it, residents of these areas "were not generally wards of the state. Rather than being indolent 'welfare cheaters,' they took responsibility for their own lives, demonstrating pride, independence, and strength.... Contrary to scholars' and reformers' descriptions of disorder and pathology," they were "able to maintain their old cultural patterns in the new environment, adapting and adjusting them when necessary." Borchert credits this state of affairs to the extensive family, self-help, and mutual-aid "safety net" of the slums.[118]

From Mutual Aid to the Welfare State[119]
Although historians have barely begun to document (or indeed fully to confirm) the decline of mutual aid, one fact is clear. The fraternal society, a key component of mutual aid, has suffered dramatic losses in membership among both the poor and the middle class. For the white insurance societies, the most accessible, although incomplete, figures are from the National Fraternal Congress (NFC). In 1906, NFC member societies represented 91,434 lodges; by 1925, they reached their apogee at 120,000 lodges. After that, the number of lodges leveled off and fell. The pace of descent quickened slightly during the Depression and then accelerated rapidly after World War II. By 1986, only

52,655 lodges remained. During the 1970s alone, the NFC lost more than 20 percent of its member lodges. Although some weathered the storm better than others, the leading white secret societies, including the Masons, the Odd Fellows and the Knights of Pythias also suffered major reverses.[120]

Tracing the longitudinal fortunes of African American mutual-aid institutions is a harder task. When compared to their white counterparts, the statistics are spotty indeed. By most, if admittedly impressionistic, measures, overall membership peaked in the 1920s and then fell during the Depression. The best known African American order, the Prince Hall Masons, recovered somewhat in the 1940s and 1950s, only to decline again in the 1960s.[121]

Even so, during and well after the Depression, African American fraternal societies maintained remarkable strength. In 1934, sociologist Guy Johnson observed that there "is scarcely a Negro community in the South that does not offer Negroes two or more kinds of church affiliation and from two to twenty brands of secret fraternal affiliation." Ten years later, Gunnar Myrdal's landmark study *An American Dilemma: The Negro Problem and Modern Democracy* asserted that African Americans of all classes were more likely than whites to join social organizations, such as fraternal societies. He estimated that over 4,000 associations in Chicago catered to the needs of the city's 275,000 African Americans.[122]

Instead of praising this high level of African American social organization, Myrdal saw it as a vice. He branded African American fraternal societies as hopeless imitations of their white counterparts and as reflective of social pathology. Myrdal declared that "despite the fact that they are predominantly lower class, Negroes are more inclined to join associations than are whites; in this respect again, Negroes are 'exaggerated' Americans." For Myrdal, the greater part of African American social organization represented "wasted effort." One wonders if Myrdal would have revised his comments could he have foreseen the isolated individual existence of the typical tenant of today's inner-city public housing projects.[123]

At this point, the state of the research does not offer easy answers to the important question of why fraternal and other mutual-aid institutions have lost so much ground in the last half-century or more. The literature has been cursory and suggestive at best. The most prevalent theories of fraternal decline stress the role of actuarial problems, originating in the faulty assessment basis of most societies formed between 1870 and 1910. Originally, it was common practice for all members, regardless of risk or age, to pay the same premium. While this system worked well initially, it came under severe strain when the membership aged. As mortality increased, higher and often onerous assessments had to be levied, leading younger (lower-risk) members to drop out. After the 1910s, the larger societies began an often painful transition to premium systems based on risk. The states adopted legislation to speed along the readjustment process, however, and the end result was to force many of the smaller, often African American, societies (which *could* still operate efficiently on an assessment basis) out of business.[124]

Richard de Raismes Kip, J. Owen Stalson, and others identify entertainment competition from radio, movies, and television as contributing to the membership losses of fraternal societies. This has some merit for explaining the fate of secret societies but works less well when applied to fraternal insurance societies. After all, the key selling-point of such societies (at least as reflected in their ads for new members) was insurance. Moreover, the focus on entertainment fails to explain why so many workers before the 1920s joined fraternal insurance societies instead of non-insurance social clubs and secret societies that were available. And if entertainment was the key attraction of fraternal membership, then why the countless efforts to institute and maintain often quite expensive insurance programs?[125]

Other factors in the decline were legal or coercive impediments which constrained fraternal societies from effectively countering new private and governmental competitors. By the 1920s, medical societies, fortified by restrictive licensing and certification barriers, had largely won (at least temporarily) their relentless battle against lodge and other forms of contract practice. The effect was not only to raise the overall cost of medical care but to close off the promising health-insurance market to further fraternal expansion.[126]

A thought-provoking variation on the theme of legislative interference has been presented by Roger L. Ransom and Richard Sutch. They contend that legal prohibitions by the states of certain insurance forms, such as the tontine policy—a form of individual old-age insurance—encouraged consumer dependency on employer benefit plans and government programs such as Social Security. Despite its promise, Ransom and Sutch's theory needs far more fleshing out.[127]

Much the same can be said for explanations positing a causal relationship between the rise of the welfare state and the decline of mutual aid. It is fairly clear that among whites and African Americans, weakened mutual aid coincided with the growth of government's social-welfare role. Government involvement in social welfare (beyond, of course, the traditional almshouse) predated the New Deal. Most states, at the onset of the Depression, already had adopted workers' compensation laws and mothers' pensions. In 1913, twenty states had mothers' pensions; by 1931 the total had reached forty-six states. The 1930s brought the first substantial federal involvement in social welfare, including Social Security and Aid to Dependent Children (ADC).[128]

Even though the correlation between rising governmental involvement and declining mutual aid is clear, a cause-and-effect relationship remains to be proven. Nevertheless, common sense, if nothing else, dictates further inquiries into possible connections between these two trends. Mutual aid, throughout history, had been a creature of necessity. Government, by taking on social welfare responsibilities that were once the ken of voluntary institutions, must have undermined much of this necessity. On this point, there are ample, and tantalizing, tidbits of circumstantial evidence for historians to chew on. With the advent of workers' compensation in the 1910s and 1920s, mutual benefit societies organized in the workplace by employees withdrew *en masse* from providing industrial accident insurance. Moreover, because workers' compensation funds flowed directly into employer-selected medical plans, the effect may have been to imperil competing services offered by fraternal societies.[129]

Paradoxically, although he defends the welfare state, Katz speculates that government transfer programs contributed to a substantial decline in mutual aid among the poor. He acknowledges that before the advent of the welfare state, the poor relied on "a series of complex, intersecting networks" based on "intimate chains of reciprocity and spontaneous and extraordinary acts of generosity between poor people themselves," and cites federal welfare initiatives as factors that "may have weakened [these] networks of support within inner cities, transforming the experience of poverty and fueling the rise of homelessness."[130]

The relationship, if any, between the decline of mutual aid and the recent fortunes of the family, another central social-welfare institution, also bears further examination. In contrast to the sparse historical literature on fraternal societies, the history of the African American family has been a favored research topic since the 1960s. The best known recent study remains Herbert Gutman's *The Black Family in Slavery and Freedom, 1750–1925* (1976). Gutman disputed Daniel Patrick Moynihan's 1965 study (still popular in some circles), which concluded that the experience of slavery had left the African American family hopelessly "disorganized" and unable to cope with social change. Using census records from a wide range of localities, Gutman found that at least until the 1920s, African American families were about as likely as white families to be headed by two parents. While African Americans had more children outside of marriage than whites, it was the accepted practice to incorporate single parents and their children into the family system. In 1983, by contrast, 41.9 percent of African American families had no husband present. As Gutman's study indicates, the current high incidence of single-parent households in African American families appears to be a product of the twentieth century, not a legacy of slavery.[131]

While important, the current rarity of the two-parent form among impoverished African Americans does not, by itself, represent a clear-cut index of increased family breakdown. Recent scholars of the African American family have aptly pointed out that one-parent or loosely extended family forms have functioned perfectly well in some historical contexts. A more precise indicator of "breakdown" that lacks normative connotations would be the degree to which a family (whatever its composition) has become dependent for its livelihood on nonreciprocal relationships and institutions. By this measure, of course, considerable family breakdown has occurred since the Depression era. The most glaring facet of increased family dependence on outside sources (as opposed to self-help and mutual-aid institutions such as the fraternal society) has been a mushrooming welfare case load. In 1931, 93,000 families were on the mothers' pension rolls (well under 1 percent of the US population). By comparison, 3.8 million families now receive AFDC, including about one-fifth of the entire African American population.[132]

The shift from mutual aid and self-help to the welfare state involved more than just a simple bookkeeping transfer of service provision from one set of institutions to another. As the leaders of fraternal societies had feared, much was lost in the exchange that transcended monetary calculations. The old relationships of reciprocity and autonomy that fraternal societies had exemplified were slowly replaced by paternalistic ties of dependency. The rise of the welfare state not only accompanied the eclipse of indigenously controlled mutual-aid institutions, but left impersonal bureaucracies dominated by outsiders in their place.[133]

Section III

The Welfare State, the Financial Crisis, and the Debt Crisis

The Welfare State as a Pyramid Scheme

By Michael Tanner

Pay-As-You-Go (PAYGO) financing can be an attractive option for politicians who know that they will retire before the system collapses. As the system matures it reaches a point where the number of beneficiaries grows and the number of workers paying into the system declines, leaving increasing gaps between state income and expenditure. Governmental pension systems and governmental financing or management of health care around the world are now approaching the point of collapse. The unfunded liabilities will place enormous and unsustainable burdens on today's young people. Michael Tanner is a senior fellow at the Cato Institute and author of several books, including Leviathan on the Right: How Big Government Brought Down the Republican Revolution *and* The Poverty of Welfare: Helping Others in Civil Society.

Margaret Thatcher once quipped about the problem facing modern social welfare states: "They always run out of other people's money." Today, in country after country, we are seeing that prophetic remark coming true. The headlines have been dominated by the problems of the so-called PIIGS (Portugal, Ireland, Italy, Greece, and Spain), which face the most immediate economic crisis. However, even countries with relatively robust economies, such as France and Germany, are facing unprecedented levels of debt. In 2010, France ran a deficit equal to 7.1 percent of GDP, while Germany's deficit hit 4.3 percent of GDP, despite not having engaged in as much expensive stimulus measures as other countries in response to the recession. Deficits add to the total of the government debt that must be serviced each year. France's debt was 81.7 percent of GDP; Germany's 83.2 percent. Britain's debt topped 68 percent of GDP. In fact, Britain's debt is rising so quickly that by 2040 interest payments alone will consume 27 percent of the country's GDP.

To put this in perspective, every working person in Germany shoulders €42,000 ($52,565) in debt. Britain's national debt is a staggering £90,000 ($140,322) per household. Every man, woman, and child in France is burdened with a €24,000 ($30,037) debt.

And all those measures may significantly understate the real level of debt facing those countries since they do not include the unfunded liabilities of their state pension (or social security) systems. Across the EU, those unfunded pension liabilities now average 285 percent of GDP. In some countries, the future liabilities are so enormous as to be nearly beyond comprehension. For example, if Greece were to fully account for its future unfunded pension obligations its total debt would exceed 875 percent of its GDP, nearly nine times the value of everything produced every year in the country. In France total debt rises to 549 percent once all of its current pension promises are taken into account, while in Germany the total debt level would soar to 418 percent if unfunded pension liabilities were fully accounted for.

Such "budgetary imbalances" (the present value of the difference between what governments are projected to spend and what they expect to receive in revenue) will lead to some combination of staggering tax increases, repudiation of obligations (either debt or promised benefits or both), or indirect repudiation through waves of inflation, as central banks create money to close the gap and to erode the value of the debt and other obligations. (Such inflation has numerous harmful effects, besides placing a disproportionate portion of the burden on the poor, who are least able to protect themselves from the "inflation tax.") Richard Disney of the University of Nottingham estimates that if current social welfare policies remain unchanged, European nations will be forced to raise taxes by 5 to 15 percentage points of GDP (not by 5 to 15 percent over current levels, but 5 to 15 *percentage points* of GDP) just to avoid an increase in debt. That would mean tax rates running from 45 to 60 percent of GDP. And that would simply avoid *new* debt, not pay off any *existing* debt.

In short, European countries cannot tax their way out of this crisis.

As frightening as the numbers discussed above may be, to focus on taxes and debt is to confuse the symptoms with the disease. As Milton Friedman often explained, the real issue is not how you pay for government spending—debt or taxes—but the spending itself.

Today, the average EU government consumes slightly more than 52 percent of the country's GDP. And, while government spending does not precisely equate to the welfare state—government, after all, performs various functions—social welfare spending makes up a growing proportion of spending for most European governments. Transfer payments are now the single largest category of economic expenditure in most EU countries, and overall social welfare spending represents more than 42 percent of all EU government spending. Debt is the symptom and the welfare state is the cause.

The United States is not in significantly better shape. In fact, only two European countries, Greece and Ireland, have larger budget deficits as a percentage of GDP. Things are only slightly better when you look at the size of the US national debt, which now exceeds $15.3 trillion, 102 percent of GDP. Just four European countries have larger national debts than does the US—Greece and Ireland again, plus Portugal and Italy. If one adds the unfunded liabilities of Social Security and Medicare to the officially acknowledged national debt, the US really owes $72 trillion, according to the conservative numbers from the Obama administration's projections for future Medicare savings under Obamacare, but more realistic projections go as high as $137 trillion. So even under the best-case scenario, then, that amounts to more than 480 percent of GDP. And, under more realistic projections, the US budgetary imbalance may reach 911 percent of GDP. The situations in Greece and in the US may not be so different, after all.

And, while the welfare state gripping the US may not yet be as large as Europe's, it is growing rapidly. Currently, the US federal government spends more than 24 percent of GDP. That is projected to rise to 42 percent of GDP by 2050. Add state and local government spending, and government at all levels will exceed 59 percent of GDP, higher than any country in Europe today.

Yet, as the economist Herbert Stein famously noted, "Whenever something cannot go on forever, it will stop." The modern welfare state cannot simply continue to chase ever-higher spending with ever-higher taxes. Nor can countries such as Greece, Portugal, Italy, and Spain continue to rely on bailouts from relatively better-off countries such as France and Germany, since eventually those countries too will have to face their own mounting debts and unfunded liabilities.

Fortunately, there are alternatives to the welfare state. Take, for example, the three largest components of most welfare states: old-age pensions, health care, and care for the poor. Free markets provide more affordable—and more effective—ways to achieve those goals.

For instance, government-run old-age pension programs, which transfer money from current workers to current retirees, are becoming increasingly unaffordable in the face of aging societies. Such systems are often politically popular when they're established because they're financed on a "Pay-As-You-Go" (PAYGO) basis and have the same financial structure as a "pyramid scheme." As the number of retirees receiving benefits grows, and the number of workers supporting them declines, the system collapses. To avoid such collapse, governments could shift away from PAYGO transfer programs to systems in which individuals save for their own retirement through private investment in the wealth-producing economy.

Americans are told that their payroll taxes are "invested" in a "trust fund," but it's nothing more than an IOU from the federal government to pay benefits in the future from future taxes. There is no "investment" at all; when the system runs surpluses of revenue over expenditure, the revenue is "borrowed" to pay for current government expenditures and a government bond— an "IOU" to tax future workers—is put in its place. The day of reckoning, when expenditures exceed revenues and those IOUs will be redeemed in additional taxes, is just a few years away.

More and more governments have come to realize that state pension plans are unsound, unfair, and unsustainable. Today, more than 30 nations have begun reforming their pension programs by allowing workers to save and invest at least a portion of what they had previously paid in payroll taxes.

A broad and growing trend in countries with national health care systems is to move away from centralized government control, which promotes queues, rising costs, limited access, and rationing, and to introduce more market-oriented features, including greater competition, customer choice, and non-tax financing. Countries such as Switzerland, and to a lesser extent the Netherlands and France, are loosening government controls and injecting market mechanisms, including cost-sharing by patients, market pricing of goods and services, and increased competition among insurers and providers.

Programs targeted at the poor remain the area where most governments have not yet begun to make reforms. Some, of course, have been forced to cut back on the level of support that they provide, and some have begun making some benefits conditional, requiring recipients, for example, to work or at least to seek employment. However, few have seriously rethought the idea of government primacy in caring for those in need.

Yet serious reform is needed. It is not merely a question of financing those programs at a time when governments simply don't have the money. Beyond the monetary cost, those programs are eroding the social structures necessary to prosperous and cooperative societies. Rather than ending poverty, the effect of income transfers, government housing, and other means-tested programs is to foster and perpetuate underclasses of people who are unable to care for themselves. Such underclasses cannot contribute to the growth needed to produce the resources that fund the very programs on which they rely.

Gradually, the responsibility for welfare should be shifted from governments to civil society, notably mutual-aid associations, self-help, and charities for the truly needy. Mutual-aid associations and charities have done a far better job of helping people to cope with misfortune, acquire skills, and escape poverty. It is one of the tragedies of the modern welfare state that those organizations have been squeezed out and replaced by the state.

One can debate the success or failure of the welfare state in meeting the needs of its citizens. What is not debatable is that the welfare state is no longer affordable. It is time to look for alternatives that won't bankrupt future generations. Fortunately, there are voluntary alternatives that do a much better job of protecting the vulnerable in our society. Citizens and governments everywhere should begin the transition from coercive, paternalistic, manipulative, and unsustainable welfare states to voluntary solutions that are effective, fair, efficient, and sustainable.

How the Right to "Affordable Housing" Created the Bubble that Crashed the World Economy

By Johan Norberg

Swedish economist and historian Johan Norberg shows how government policies designed to make housing "more affordable" created a massive housing bubble and a resulting collapse of the global financial system. Norberg is a senior fellow of the Cato Institute, author of numerous books, including När människan skapade världen (When Mankind Created the World) *and* In Defense of Global Capitalism, *and producer of several video documentaries, including "Globalization is Good" for UK Channel 4 and "Overdose: The Next Financial Crisis." This essay is extracted from chapter two of his book* Financial Fiasco: How America's Infatuation with Home Ownership and Easy Money Created the Economic Crisis (*Washington, DC: Cato Institute, 2009*), *which presents in much fuller detail the story of how a cascade of manipulative state interventions into markets—including easy money from the Federal Reserve, governmentally promoted "creative financing" for home loans, securitization of mortgages by Government-Sponsored Enterprises (Fannie Mae and Freddie Mac), and banking regulations that encouraged acquisition of risky securities—resulted in a global financial collapse.*

> *"Come to see victory*
> *In a land called fantasy"*

> —From a song by *Earth, Wind, and Fire*,
> who entertained at the big 2006 Christmas party of the
> Federal National Mortgage Association (Fannie Mae)

When Fannie Mae and Freddie Mac collapsed in 2008, the Bush administration quickly circulated the story of how it had seen the problems coming years ago and had tried to gain control over operations but how the Democrats in Congress blocked the attempt. White House officials even penned a talking-points memo entitled "GSEs—We Told You So." It described a 2003 report from Armando Falcon Jr. at the Office of Federal Housing Enterprise Oversight, whose job it was to keep an eye on Fannie and Freddie, where he warned that the two government-sponsored enterprises engaged in such irresponsible lending practices and risk management that they could become insolvent. According to Falcon, this could have a domino effect, causing liquidity shortages in the market.

There was just one small detail that Bush's aides left out of their talking-points memo: The same day that Falcon published his report, he received a call from the White House personnel department informing him that he was fired.[134]

President Bush's aim was to create an "ownership society" where citizens would be in control of their own lives and wealth through ownership, which would promote both independence and responsibility. But that did not just mean free markets based on private property rights—it was the expression of a willingness to use the levers of government to treat ownership more favorably than other contractual relationships in the marketplace. One of Bush's key objectives was to increase the proportion of homeownership, and two of his best friends in that endeavor were called Fannie and Freddie.

One sunny day in June 2002, President Bush visited the home of police officer Darrin West in Park Place South, a poor neighborhood of Atlanta, Georgia. Officer West had just been able to buy a house there thanks to a government loan that covered his down payment. The president had dropped in on him to explain the problem of blacks and Latinos not owning their homes to the same extent as whites, and to tell him what he proposed to do about it. The number of members of various minority groups who owned their homes would be 5.5 million higher by 2010, and that would be achieved by means of Fannie, Freddie, federal loans, and government subsidies. In Bush's own words:

It means we use the mighty muscle of the federal government in combination with state and local governments to encourage owning your own home.[135]

Indeed, the Republicans endorsed virtually all the decisions made by Democratic officials Henry Cisneros and Andrew Cuomo—and upped the ante. Bush designed new federal subsidies for first-time buyers, whom he wanted to be covered by federal insurance even if they did not deposit a single cent as down payment. In 2004, it was time to set new targets for the government-sponsored enterprises. Cisneros had demanded that 42 percent of Fannie's and Freddie's mortgages go to low-income earners, and Cuomo had raised that to 50 percent. The Bush administration raised it once more, stipulating 56 percent in 2008. An even more remarkable change was that the proportion of loans to be made to people with very low incomes was to increase from 20 percent all the way up to 28 percent.

"No one wanted to stop that bubble," according to Lawrence Lindsey, Bush's senior economic aide. "It would have conflicted with the president's own policies."[136] And to some extent, housing policy had acquired a momentum of its own. As more people could get mortgages more easily, more of them entered the housing market and prices went up. That in turn made it more difficult for those who had not yet ventured into that market to afford a home, meaning that new political interventions were required to make it even easier to get a mortgage, which pushed prices even higher. And yet the huge mortgages looked harmless, exactly because prices kept rising and you could easily take out a new loan on your old home.

The administration's attitude toward Fannie and Freddie did not begin to change until after a startling scandal. In June 2003, only a few months after its regulators had declared Freddie Mac's accounts "accurate and reliable," it was revealed that the enterprise had stashed away profits of $6.9 billion in the previous three years for use in harder times. Scrutiny of the government-sponsored enterprises' accounts then showed that Fannie Mae had cooked its books, too, but by overstating profits to ensure that its bosses would get their full bonuses. A series of other irregularities was also exposed, and the senior executives were sent packing.

It came as a shock that the GSEs, seen by many as a type of charitable society—President Bush liked to say that they did business from their hearts—appeared to have learned their bookkeeping skills from Enron, the energy firm that imploded in 2001. Only a few days before the scandal at Freddie Mac broke, its supervisor, the Office of Federal Housing Enterprise Oversight (OFHEO), had stated the following in a report to Congress:

> Freddie Mac's proprietary risk management programs and systems are effective. Management effectively conveys an appropriate message of integrity and ethical values. Management's philosophy and operating style have a pervasive effect on the company. The organizational structure and the assignment of responsibility provide for accountability and controls.[137]

Now the OFHEO had to talk about large-scale fraud at the government-sponsored enterprises instead, and it fined them more than half-a-billion dollars. The accounting scams strengthened Fannie's and Freddie's skeptics in the Bush administration. Alan Greenspan sharply criticized them for exposing the economy to risk, and President Bush reinstated Armando Falcon Jr., the critic of Fannie and Freddie who had in fact been fired, in his job as their supervisor. The administration decided to tighten supervision of the two enterprises and wanted a bank-like receivership process in the event of a crisis that would stipulate that the federal government did not guarantee all their liabilities. This would have dealt a disastrous blow to the enterprises' business model, which was built solely on the "big, fat gap" (in Greenspan's words[138]) between the cheap interest rates at which they could borrow thanks to the federal guarantee and the market rates they earned on their lending.

But the administration would not get the last word. At an investors' meeting in 1999, Fannie Mae's CEO Franklin Raines had declared, "We manage our political risk with the same intensity that we manage our credit and interest rate risks."[139] If anything, that was an understatement. As Fannie was progressively losing control of the mortgages it bought, it devoted more and more time and money to monitoring all political threats to its financial position. Over the years, it had also used its profits to build a lobbying organization with local offices and a network of politicians that few institutions could match. In the past decade, Fannie has spent $170 million on lobbying and donations to political candidates.[140] Fannie and Freddie often hired politicians' relatives to work at their local offices, and friendly politicians could themselves find well-paid employment with the government-sponsored enterprises during periods when they were out of elected office. In exchange for political support, Fannie and Freddie regularly let members of Congress announce large housing developments for low-income earners—in practice, political decisions that never had to pass through political decision-making processes. By contrast, members of Congress who wanted to whittle down the privileges of Fannie or Freddie would be drowned in angry calls and letters, and voters would receive automatic phone messages: "Your congressman is trying to make mortgages more expensive. Ask him why he opposes the American dream of homeownership."[141]

The strategy had been outstandingly successful, and the critics of the two enterprises had been beaten back time and again. In 1999, President Clinton's Treasury secretary Lawrence Summers was concerned about Fannie and Freddie, but his reform proposal was shot down. They could even flout the rules of the New York Stock Exchange, under which a corporation that does not present annual reports on its financial position must be removed from trading. When Fannie failed to do so, the NYSE introduced an exemption—applicable if "delisting would be significantly contrary to the national interest." The Securities and Exchange Commission approved the exemption, and Fannie Mae could remain listed.[142]

One of those who got a taste of Fannie's and Freddie's wrath was Rep. Richard Baker (R-LA), who had obtained information in 2003 from their supervisory authority about how much they paid their top executives. Fannie and Freddie threatened to sue him if he went public with the information, which made him keep it under his hat for a year. Baker, who has now left Congress, told the *Washington Post* that he had never experienced anything like it: "The political arrogance exhibited in their heyday, there has never been before or since a private entity that exerted that kind of political power."[143]

When the Bush administration had turned its back on them, Fannie and Freddie set their entire lobbying machine in motion to mount a violent attack on the reform proposals. They mobilized the housing and real-estate finance industry and activist groups they had often donated money to, and they went for a large-scale advertising campaign on TV and radio. "But that could mean we won't be able to afford the new house," a dejected woman in one of the TV spots concluded about the consequences of the proposals. Fannie and Freddie won. The Democrats put up strong resistance, managing to remove the receivership provisions from the House bill, leading the bill to become so watered down that the administration no longer wanted to support it. In the Senate, Robert Bennett (R-UT) managed to weaken the provisions regarding securities disclosures and capital requirements.

Senator Bennett's second-largest donor was Fannie Mae. His son worked for Fannie in Utah.

Anybody Could Have Seen It Coming

To Fannie Mae and Freddie Mac, their defeat of the Bush administration was as costly as the Greek commander Pyrrhus's original Pyrrhic victory over the Romans at Asculum. They used to enjoy broad support from both political parties, but now that the administration had turned against them, they had to rely more and more on the congressional Democrats, who wanted even faster expansion of the two enterprises' most popular operation: loans to low-income earners and minorities. Fannie and Freddie's only chance of survival was to cultivate the Democrats' support by letting go of all restraint with regard to credit checks and lending. They had also lost time because of the accounting scandals, which had allowed other lenders to take market share from them. And at this point, most low-income earners who could handle a mortgage on normal market terms had already got one long ago. The government-sponsored enterprises therefore had to venture into even riskier territory in their attempt to regain lost ground.

Daniel Mudd, the CEO of Fannie Mae, left no doubt about the future strategy. He told his workers to "get aggressive on risk-taking, or get out of the company." A former employee explained to the *New York Times* that everybody knew they had started buying mortgages in an unsustainable way, "but our mandate was to stay relevant and to serve low-income borrowers. So that's what we did."[144] In mid-2004, Freddie Mac's chief risk officer David Andrukonis told the CEO Richard Syron that credit checks had become increasingly lax and risked exposing both the enterprise and the country to great financial risks. But Syron refused to heed the warnings, explaining dejectedly to Andrukonis that Freddie Mac could no longer afford to say no to anybody.[145]

Even though the Bush administration had criticized Fannie and Freddie for their reckless risk taking, it inexplicably helped drive them further down that road by decreeing in October 2004, at the height of the lending craze, a drastic *increase* in their targets for the number of mortgages to low-income earners. As previously mentioned, the share of such mortgages was to increase each year, from 50 percent in 2000 to 56 percent in 2008. The share of loans to people on very low incomes was to rise from 20 to 28 percent.

There was a defeatist atmosphere at Fannie Mae and Freddie Mac even at that point. Their senior executives had given up trying to serve all their masters: the stockholders' demands for long-term profitability could not be reconciled with the politicians' directives to step on the gas. One employee described how discussions at the office would increasingly be about how long it would take before they were exposed:

> It didn't take a lot of sophistication to notice what was happening to the quality of the loans. Anybody could have seen it. But nobody on the outside was even questioning us about it.[146]

In fact, there were political reasons for not wanting to see what was going on. The intentions were good, and the objectives were almost beyond criticism. As late as July 2008, Paul Krugman, a leftwing economist who would soon win the Nobel Prize, attacked the critics of Fannie and Freddie, pointing out that the duo had nothing to do with risky lending and had not made a single subprime loan.[147] Krugman may have been mixing things up: It is true that Fannie and Freddie did not lend to subprime borrowers, because they did not lend at all; but they did buy loans, and a growing share of those loans were subprime. But Fannie and Freddie also tried to cover up their risky lending by applying narrower definitions of "subprime" than most other players in the market. In July 2007, the chief risk officer of Countrywide proudly told analysts during a conference call that his institution was selling mortgages to Fannie Mae that were "far below" even generous limits for subprime but that were still considered "prime" by Fannie.[148]

The message sent out by Fannie and Freddie around 2004 that they would be buying just about anything that moved was a large part of the reason banks and other institutions started pumping out new mortgages that were subprime and Alt-A. "The market knew we needed those loans," a Freddie Mac spokesperson explained.[149] "Alt-A" was a type of loan considered riskier than "prime" but less risky than "subprime." Since loans were often given this label because there was no documentation of the borrower's income, another name for them is "liar loans." In practice, they turned out to be about as risky as subprime loans, and it has been suggested that subprime and Alt-A should be merged into the less opaquely named category of "junk loans." In 2003, junk loans accounted for only 8 percent of all US mortgages, but that increased to 18 percent in 2004 and to as much as 22 percent in the third quarter of 2006. About 40 percent of the mortgages that Fannie and Freddie bought in 2005–2007 were subprime or Alt-A.[150]

The grandiose objectives had forced Fannie and Freddie to change their strategy. Instead of just buying mortgages and repackaging them into securities, they now bought more and more such securities from others. In fact, Fannie and Freddie soon became the largest buyers of the safest "tranche"—that is, the specific group with the highest credit rating—of each such security. Many commentators think that was decisive for the uncontrolled spread of subprime mortgage securities across the world. The reason is that the yield on the safest tranche was barely higher than the interest paid by banks on deposits, meaning that investors were not exactly lining up to buy. But to Fannie and Freddie, which were able to borrow cheaply because of their government backing, it could still look like an attractive deal. And once they had supplied capital for that tranche, it was easier to find other investors who were willing to buy the riskier ones, which yielded much bigger returns—sometimes up to 20 times more. That prompted companies such as New Century and Ameriquest to design securities solely to make Fannie and Freddie buy them: it was no coincidence that the amount of the mortgages those securities were based on was just below $417,000, which was the ceiling for loans that could be part of Fannie's and Freddie's portfolios.[151]

Fannie's and Freddie's joint exposure to the housing market was huge. At the end of 2007, the sum of the liabilities and mortgage-backed securities that they had guaranteed and issued equaled the US national debt. For every $100 they had guaranteed or lent through securities, they had only $1.20 of equity.[152] In August 2008, Fannie and Freddie owned junk loans and securities based on junk loans worth over $1 trillion—more than one-fifth of their entire mortgage portfolio.[153] In the words of Nassim Nicholas Taleb, author of the book *The Black Swan,* about how people underestimate low-probability risks, they were "sitting on a barrel of dynamite." Their army of analysts, however, claimed that the risks were small. They had sophisticated models to manage risks. That is, all risks but one—a fall in home prices.[154]

As Freddie Mac's former CEO Richard Syron looked back on what went wrong, he blamed the bad mortgages on politicians' pushing through an expansion of homeownership even to households that could not afford to own a home. That was the price the government-sponsored enterprises had to pay for their privileges. But 15 years earlier, it had been on Syron's watch that the Boston Fed had started its systematic efforts to loosen banks' requirements for creditworthiness, and at Freddie Mac, he had led a huge expansion of the subprime market. When the *New York Times* recently asked him if there was nothing he could have done differently, he replied: "If I had better foresight, maybe I could have improved things a little bit. But frankly, if I had perfect foresight, I would never have taken this job in the first place."[155]

Section IV

Poverty and the Welfare State

Poverty, Morality, and Liberty

By Tom G. Palmer

The understanding of poverty and appropriate solutions to it has evolved over centuries. This essay draws on moral philosophy, economics, history, and other disciplines to review the nature and sources of poverty and wealth, as they have been understood by classical liberals, and to lay out their view of the proper role of self-help, mutual aid, charity, and state compulsion in the alleviation of poverty. A longer version of this essay was first published in the book Poverty and Morality: Religious and Secular Perspectives (*Cambridge: Cambridge University Press, 2010*), *edited by Peter Hoffenberg and William A. Galston.*

"Classical liberalism" and "libertarianism" refer to that tradition of ethical, political, legal, and economic thought that places the freedom of the individual at the center of political concern and that sees that freedom as, in John Locke's language, each person's enjoyment of a *"Liberty* to dispose, and order, as he lists, his Persons, Actions, Possessions, and his whole Property, within the Allowance of those Laws under which he is; and therein not to be subject to the arbitrary Will of another, but freely follow his own."[156]

Classical liberals, despite often vigorous disagreement among themselves over both the foundations of liberty and the proper limits on state power, have generally agreed on the thesis of the presumption of liberty; that is, that it is interference with the freedom of others that must be justified, and not their free action itself. The exercise of power requires justification; the exercise of liberty does not.[157]

Three commonly accepted core elements of classical liberal thought are:

1. A conviction, expressed in many different ways, that "individuals have rights and that there are things no person or group may do to them (without violating their rights)"[158];
2. An appreciation for the capacity for social order and harmony to emerge spontaneously, without the conscious direction of any mind or the imposition of any plan, as an unintended consequence of people interacting freely on the basis of rights (property) that are well defined, defendable, and structured by legal rules facilitating contract;
3. A commitment to constitutionally limited government that is authorized to enforce the rules of just conduct but is strictly limited in its powers.

Thus, the tradition of classical liberal thinking draws primarily from three disciplines—moral philosophy, social science, and political (or juridical) science, supplemented by ancillary disciplines such as psychology, history, and sociology. Each of the three elements reinforces the others to produce a coherent theory of the relationship of freedom, rights, government, and order.

Adam Smith, a doyen of the classical liberal tradition and a contributor to all three of those primary disciplines—moral philosophy (*The Theory of Moral Sentiments*), social science (*An Inquiry into the Nature and Causes of the Wealth of Nations*), and political or juridical science (*The Lectures on Jurisprudence*)—connected all three pillars in a famous statement:

Little else is requisite to carry a state to the highest degree of opulence from the lowest barbarism, but peace, easy taxes, and a tolerable administration of justice; all the rest being brought about by the natural course of things. All governments which thwart this natural course, which force things into another channel, or which endeavour to arrest the progress of society at a particular point, are unnatural, and to support themselves are obliged to be oppressive and tyrannical.[159]

Definitions

Classical liberalism has had a long engagement with the issue of poverty, partly because of its intimate association with economic science in particular and the study of spontaneous forms of social order and improvement in general. Classical liberals have insisted that the question of the "wealth of nations" comes logically before "the poverty of nations." Poverty is meaningful only in comparison to wealth, and wealth must be produced. Poverty is the natural base line against which wealth is measured; poverty is what you have if wealth is not produced. The classical liberal economist Peter Bauer of the London School of Economics famously retorted to John Kenneth Galbraith's discussion of the "causes of poverty": "Poverty has no causes. Wealth has causes." As the historians Nathan Rosenberg and L. E. Birdzell Jr. put the matter, "If we take the long view of human history and judge the economic lives of our ancestors by modern standards, it is a story of almost unrelieved wretchedness."[160] Widespread poverty is the historical norm; the wealth explosion of the past two centuries is the aberration that requires explanation.

Prosperity, as it is understood today, is a uniquely modern phenomenon. The experience of the great bulk of the human race for most of its existence, up until quite recently, has been the experience of early death, sickness, ignorance, almost unrelieved physical toil, and uncertain access to sufficient food to sustain life. The picture of the past commonly carried by so many intellectuals is deeply misleading, as it is derived almost entirely from the writings of other intellectuals, that is, from that tiny minority fortunate enough to enjoy the leisure to write about their lives. Such accounts are hardly representative of the lives of the great bulk of the human race. The difference between the material conditions of existence that characterized most of the human past and now is substantial. In the words of classical liberal economic historian Deirdre McCloskey,

> The heart of the matter is twelve. Twelve is the factor by which real income per head nowadays exceeds that around 1780, in Britain and in other countries that have experienced modern economic growth.

... Most conservatively measured, the average person has about twelve times more bread, books, transport and innocent amusement than the average person had two centuries ago. No previous episode of enrichment approaches modern economic growth—not China or Egypt in their primes, not the glory of Greece or the grandeur of Rome.[161]

Table 1

Levels of GDP Per Capita in European Colonial Powers and Former Colonies, 1500–1998 (1990 international dollars)

	1500	1700	1820	1913	1950	1998
Britain	762	1,405	2,121	5,150	6,907	18,714
France	727	986	1,230	3,485	5,270	19,556
Italy	1,100	1,100	1,117	2,564	3,502	17,759
Netherlands	754	2,110	1,821	4,049	5,996	20,224
Portugal	632	854	963	1,244	2,069	12,929
Spain	698	900	1,063	2,255	2,397	14,227
China	600	600	600	552	439	3,117
India	550	550	533	673	619	1,746
Indonesia	565	580	612	904	840	3,070
Brazil	400	460	646	811	1,672	5,459
Mexico	425	568	759	1,732	2,365	6,655
United States	400	527	1,257	5,301	9,561	27,331
Ireland	526	715	880	2,736	3,446	18,183

Source: A. Maddison, *The World Economy*, vol. 1: *A Millennial Perspective*, and vol. 2: *Historical Statistics* (Paris: OECD, 2006), 92.

It is only the past few hundred years that have witnessed the explosion of productive energy, as shown by the enormous changes in per capita income from 1500 to 1998 (Table 1). The data are more striking when looked at graphically from the year 1 to the present (Figure 1).

The sudden and sustained rise in income from the takeoff period around the middle of the eighteenth century (for Western Europe and North America; a century or more later for others) is unprecedented in all of human history. It is the sudden shift from a nearly horizontal line to a nearly vertical line that demands explanation.

The conditions of most previous generations of humans—as judged by the standards of the present—are no less than horrifying. The focus on classical liberal historical, economic, and legal research has been on explaining the causes of that great change, and the general consensus has been that they key change was the growth of institutions conducive to the production of wealth.

Classical liberals insist that the explanation of wealth production—of what made possible the sudden trend upward in Figure 1—is primary not merely because of the suddenness of the change but also for reasons of conceptual clarity. Poverty is what results if wealth production does not take place, whereas wealth is not what results if poverty production does not take place.

Figure 1

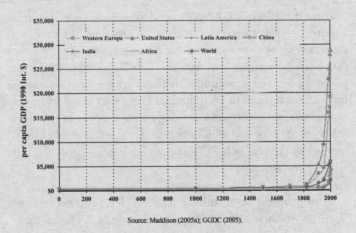

Source: Maddison (2005a); GGDC (2005).

Figure 1 Global economic development. From Indur M. Goklany, *The Improving State of the World* (Washington, DC: Cato Institute, 2007), 43.

The suddenness of the wealth explosion shown in Figure 1 is the reason that the dominant narrative in the classical liberal tradition has been one of prosperity defined against a norm of widespread poverty, not in terms of relative well-being.

Classical liberals have sought to explain the *presence of wealth* rather than taking as the fundamental puzzle its absence. The idea of a "vicious circle of poverty" as an explanation for the absence of wealth was criticized by the development economist P. T. Bauer:

> To have money is the result of economic achievement, not its precondition. That this is so is plain from the very existence of developed countries, all of which originally must have been underdeveloped and yet progressed without external donations. The world was not created in two parts, one with ready-made infrastructure and stock of capital, and the other without such facilities. Moreover, many poor countries progressed rapidly in the hundred years or so before the emergence of modern development economics and the canvassing of the vicious circle. Indeed, if the notion of the vicious circle of poverty were valid, mankind would still be living in the Old Stone Age.[162]

Almost all humans have escaped the Stone Age. In those countries that saw increases in per capita income, the effect was especially significant for the poor, whose status and even definition changed dramatically. As Carlo Cipolla noted of the impact of the "Industrial Revolution," it is undeniable that one of the main characteristics of preindustrial Europe, as of all traditional agricultural societies, was a striking contrast between the abject misery of the mass and the affluence and magnificence of a limited number of the very rich.[163] "The poor" referred to people on the verge of starvation:

> Most people lived at subsistence level. They had no savings and no social security to help them in case of distress. If they remained without work, their only hope of survival was charity. We look in vain in the language of the time for the term *unemployed*. The unemployed were confused with the poor, the poor person was identified with the beggar, and the confusion of the terms reflected the grim reality of the times. In a year of bad harvest or of economic stagnation, the number of destitute people grew conspicuously ... The

people of preindustrial times were inured to drastic fluctuations in the number of beggars. Especially in the cities the number of the poor soared in years of famine because starving peasants fled the depleted countryside and swarmed to the urban centers, where charity was more easily available and hopefully the houses of the wealthy had food in storage. Dr. Tadino reported that in Milan (Italy) during the famine of 1629 in a few months the number of beggars grew from 3,554 to 9,715. Gascon found that in Lyon (France) "in normal years the poor represented 6 to 8 percent of the population; in years of famine their number rose to 15 or 20 percent."

The fundamental characteristic of the poor was that they had no independent income. If they managed to survive, it was because income was voluntarily transferred to them through charity.[164]

The great growth of industry made the poor—in the form of large numbers of urban workers—visible to literate urban dwellers in a way that they had not been before. But no longer were they swarming masses of starving peasants hoping for alms. Their status was decidedly different. The increases in population made possible by industrialism did not arise from an increase in birth rates but from a drop in death rates, notably premature death. "If we ask," F. A. Hayek wrote, "what men most owe to the moral practices of those called capitalists the answer is: their very lives. Socialist accounts that ascribe the existence of the proletariat to an exploitation of groups formerly able to maintain themselves are entirely fictional. Most individuals who now make up the proletariat could not have existed before others provided them with means to exist."[165]

Classical liberals have persistently worked to debunk the false image of the past—common to socialists and conservatives alike, in which happy peasants gamboled on the village green, life was tranquil and unstressed, and each peasant family enjoyed a snug little cottage.[166] The common yearning for a past "golden age," a yearning that is still with us ("Ah, for the 1950s, when everyone . . ."), was described and dismissed by the classical liberal historian Thomas Babington Macaulay in the mid-nineteenth century:

> It is now the fashion to place the golden Age of England in times when noblemen were destitute of comforts the wants of which would be intolerable to a modern footman, when farmers and shopkeepers breakfasted on loaves the sight of which would raise a riot in a modern workhouse, when to have a clean shirt once a week was a privilege for the higher class of gentry.

The way of life of Macaulay's generation would today be considered unbearable by even the poorest among us, as Macaulay presciently recognized:

> We too shall, in our turn, be outstripped, and in our turn be envied. It may well be, in the twentieth century, that . . . numerous comforts and luxuries which are now unknown, or confined to a few, may be within the reach of every diligent and thrifty workingman. And yet it may then be the mode to assert that the increase of wealth and progress of science have benefited the few at the expense of many.[167]

As Macaulay understood, there is no naturally discernible dividing line between "poverty" and "wealth." The poor of today enjoy amenities unavailable to the wealthy of the past, even the relatively recent past. (If anyone doubts that, he or she should compare the experience of dentistry among the super wealthy fifty years ago with that of the poor in advanced countries today; who could doubt that the wealthy of the past would have given their eye teeth, so to speak, to enjoy the anesthesia and modern dental techniques available to even the poorest in industrial countries today?)

Comparative approaches have not been lacking in the classical liberal tradition. The Abbé de Condillac, in an influential work published in the same year as Adam Smith's *The Wealth of Nations*, distinguished between mere lack of wealth and poverty, for "there is only poverty where essential needs are not met, and it is not being poor to lack a type of wealth of which one has not acquired a need, and which one does not even know."[168] The progress of the arts and sciences and the creation of ever-greater wealth generates new needs, the satisfaction of which entails new forms of consumption.

Adam Smith added an additional element. Poverty consists not only in the consciousness of unmet need but also in the comparison of one's status with that of others in a way that causes shame. Shame is a defining feature of what is a "necessity," that is, something without which one would be accounted poor:

> By necessities I understand, not only the commodities which are indispensably necessary for the support of life, but whatever the custom of the country renders it indecent for creditable people, even of the lowest order, to be without. A linen shirt, for example, is, strictly speaking, not a necessary of life. The Greeks and Romans lived, I suppose, very comfortably, though they had no linen. But in the present times, through the greater part of Europe, a creditable day-labourer would be ashamed to appear in publick without a linen shirt, the want of which would be supposed to denote that disgraceful degree of poverty, which, it is presumed, no body can well fall into without extreme bad conduct. . . . Under necessaries therefore, I comprehend, not only those things which nature, but those things which the established rules of decency have rendered necessary to the lowest ranks of people. All other things, I call luxuries; . . . Nature does not render them necessary for the support of life; and custom no where renders it indecent to live without them.[169]

Under both absolute and comparative conceptions, wealth and poverty are moving standards. An accumulation of assets that may qualify one as wealthy in one year may, in a wealthier succeeding year, qualify one as poor, and a wealthy person in one society may be poor in another.

Consistent with their focus on wealth as the phenomenon to be explained, then, classical liberals addressed themselves assiduously to the analysis of why some fare better or worse than others.

Smith's book was famously called *An Inquiry into the Nature and Causes of the Wealth of Nations*. Most prior writers had identified the wealth of a nation (its nature) with the wealth of the ruling elite. In contrast, Smith began his work by identifying the nature of a nation's wealth, not with its military power or the gold and silver in the king's treasury, but with the annual produce of the combined labor power of the nation, divided by the number of consumers, a conception that persists in the modern notion of per capita gross domestic product.[170]

The wealth of a nation is to be measured, then, not by the power of its rulers or the bullion in the state treasury, but by the access to wealth on the part of any randomly chosen member of it: "That state is properly opulent in which opulence is easily come at, or in which a little labour, properly and judiciously employed, is capable of procuring any man a great abundance of all the necessaries and conveniencies of life."[171] The primary causes or determinants of wealth are the institutions that create incentives for wealth production. Poverty, then, as measured against a background of wealth, represents a failure to create (or hold on to) wealth, and the causes of such failure are those institutions or practices that create *dis*incentives for wealth production and/or incentives for predatory transfers that directly impoverish some for the benefit of others.

If opportunities, understood as freedoms to engage in voluntary activities to create wealth, are unequally distributed, it is likely that that will entail an unequal distribution of wealth, not because a sum of "socially created" wealth has been divided unfairly, but because the opportunities to produce wealth have been withheld from some, who as a consequence are able to produce less. Classical liberals have emphasized that every act of production is itself an act of distribution. If freedom to produce is unequal, holdings of wealth will also be unequal. For example, recipients of state grants of monopoly can charge higher prices in the absence of competition and reap monopoly rents as a consequence, a process (now known as rent-seeking) that both transfers wealth from one party to another and, in the process, diminishes the aggregate of wealth produced, as resources are diverted to rent-seeking itself and away from production of value, thus making the society as a whole less wealthy than it would have been in the absence of rent-seeking behavior.[172]

If some have the power to force others to produce not for their own benefit but for the benefit of the powerful, they will transfer wealth from the coerced to those who coerce, sometimes at a great net loss in productivity. Slavery, serfdom, conscription, and other forms of forced labor transfer wealth from some to others. Theft and other forms of involuntary transfers confiscate from some what they have produced, generally to the benefit of the confiscators.[173] Restrictions on some from competing with others generate rents to those with monopolistic powers, at the expense of their customers and potential competitors. A society in which some are forbidden by force of law from owning land, entering certain trades, or purchasing commodities at freely negotiated prices would likely see a difference in per capita income between those groups that suffered from legal disabilities and those that did not. Examples from history abound.[174]

Vulnerability to Poverty

Vulnerability to poverty is seen by classical liberals as substantially dependent on institutional settings. When there are rewards to violence or procurement of political power and force, the violent and the politically ambitious will benefit by snatching from the industrious the wealth they have produced, impoverishing the industrious and diminishing incentives for further production of wealth, to the relative impoverishment of all. The history of civilization is a history of limitations on power and violence, achieved by a variety of means.[175]

In legal orders characterized by well-defined, legally secure, and transferable property rights, with strong limitations on predatory behavior, poverty tends to be transformed from the dividing line between survival and starvation and becomes a matter of relative affluence, with the lesser affluence of the poor largely a matter of inability or unwillingness to produce wealth or to save, rather than to squander, what one has acquired. Thus, "character" (also known as possession of the virtues)[176] is a factor, as the industrious and the thrifty are in such legal orders unlikely to experience poverty, reckoned in either absolute or relative terms.

In relatively free and prosperous societies, the best predictors of relative poverty tend to be the degree to which one is a recipient of state assistance, which, they have argued, tends to foster the vices of indolence and irresponsibility. The classic example was the working of the "Poor Laws" in relatively prosperous England, and especially the "Speenhamland System" of "outdoor relief" that subsidized the working poor.[177] As Alexis de Tocqueville argued in his *Memoir on Pauperism*, written after a tour of England, the availability of "legal charity" in wealthy countries such as Britain, before the reform of the "Poor Laws," was itself a cause of poverty, for it had, he argued, created a permanent class of paupers. His investigation was aimed at resolving an apparent paradox: "The countries appearing to be most impoverished are those which in reality account for the fewest indigents, and among the people most admired for their opulence, one part of the population is obliged to live on the gifts of the other in order to live."[178]

As Tocqueville concluded from his investigation, "Any measure that establishes legal charity on a permanent basis and gives it an administrative form thereby creates an idle and lazy class, living at the expense of the industrial and working class."[179] In addition to creating incentives for some to become dependent on others, the Poor Laws created incentives for the industrious to attempt to control the movement of the recipients of "outdoor relief," lest newcomers become burdens to ratepayers. According to Tocqueville,

> Legal charity affects the pauper's freedom as much as his morality. This is easily proved. When local governments are rigorously obligated to aid the indigent, they necessarily owe relief only to the poor who reside in their jurisdiction. This is the only fair way of equalizing the public burden which results from the law, and of proportioning it to the means of those who must bear it. Since individual charity is almost unknown in a country of organized public charity, anyone whose misfortunes or vices have made him incapable of earning a living is condemned, under pain of death, to remain in the place of his birth. If he leaves, he moves through enemy territory. The private interest within the parish, infinitely

more active and powerful than the best organized national police could be, notes his arrival, dogs his every step, and, if he wants to establish a new residence, informs the public authority who takes him to the boundary line. Through their Poor Laws, the English have immobilized a sixth of their population. They have bound it to the earth like the medieval peasantry. Then, man was forced against his will to stay on the land where he was born. Legal charity keeps him from even wishing to move.[180]

A similar dynamic of control set in motion by welfare statism explains profoundly illiberal policies of restrictions on freedom of movement across international borders, as immigrants are often seen by the inhabitants of welfare states as parasites who threaten to consume the wealth of the locals, rather than as potential producers of wealth who come for mutual benefit.[181]

Institutionalization of the Political and Economic Means to Wealth Acquisition

A major—indeed, the most important—factor of production is the institutional framework that facilitates voluntary cooperation for mutual benefit. Wealth production is a result of institutional changes that create incentives for productivity and mutual gains resulting from trade. As Benjamin Friedman notes, "This bold new concept had strong moral content. For the first time people saw the possibility of acquiring wealth in a way that need not be inherently exploitive. At the individual level, the idea of voluntary exchange was that in any transaction both parties expected to come out ahead. But the same point applied even more strikingly at the level of the entire society. The route to national wealth was commerce, not conquest."[182] Following on that insight, classical liberals have distinguished two means of acquiring wealth: the "economic means" of production and exchange and the "political means" of deploying force.[183] Herbert Spencer distinguished between two ideal types of society, the "militant" and the "industrial": the former characterized by command and hierarchy and the latter by cooperation and contract.[184]

As special privileges in law will generate differences in wealth and income, classical liberals strove to identify and eliminate those special privileges that harmed some to the benefit of others.[185] Thus, classical liberals have campaigned vigorously against guild privileges that restricted entrance to trades; racial, ethnic, religious, and gender barriers to ownership of property or entry to trades; protectionist barriers to cheap imports, which raise prices to consumers to benefit small minorities of domestic producers; and a wide array of obstacles to the efforts of people to improve their situations. Legal equality, freedom of trade, and careers open to talent were watchwords of classical liberal theorists of social progress.[186]

Classical liberals prided themselves on the results of their efforts. As the classical liberal journalist E. L. Godkin noted in the pages of the *Nation* in 1900, "To the principle and precepts of Liberalism the prodigious material progress of the age was largely due. Freed from the vexatious meddling of governments, men devoted themselves to their natural task, the bettering of their condition, with the wonderful results which surround us."[187]

Wealth and Inequality

Just as classical liberals do not see poverty as "the cause" of poverty (in the "vicious circle of poverty" argument criticized by P. T. Bauer), they do not see the existence of wealth as the cause of poverty, as it is by some socialists, who argue that not giving a poor person goods and services is the "cause" of that person's poverty.[188] Voluntarily acquired wealth is, in fact, a cause of the wealth of others, not of their poverty. "Say's Law," according to which "it is production which opens a demand for products," postulated that the wealth of one person, group, or nation was to the benefit of those who traded with them.[189]

What could an active manufacturer, or an intelligent merchant, do in a small, deserted and semi-barbarous town in a remote corner of Poland or Westphalia? Though in no fear of a competitor, he could sell but little, because little was produced; whilst at Paris, Amsterdam, or London, in spite of the competition of a hundred dealers in his own line, he might do business on the largest scale. The reason is obvious: he is surrounded with people who produce largely in an infinity of ways, and who make purchases, each with his respective products, that is to say, with the money arising from the sale of what he may have produced.[190]

Institutions create incentives and incentives shape behavior. As Douglass North puts it, "Institutions provide the incentive structure of an economy; as that structure evolves, it shapes the direction of economic change towards growth, stagnation, or decline."[191]

Outcomes are not in general subject to choice; at best, one can choose one process over another, not one outcome over another. What may seem like the choice of an outcome (e.g., higher wages) is, in fact, the choice of a process (prohibiting the creation or fulfillment of labor contracts below a certain wage). Processes do not always generate the outcomes that the choosers may have hoped for. Daniel Shapiro notes that "institutions cannot be adequately characterized by their aims."[192] Thus, classical liberals have criticized a great deal of intervention into voluntary exchange on the grounds that it does not generate the outcomes promised. Minimum wage laws, for example, do not raise wages—increasing the marginal product of labor raises wages, and that is not subject to control by legislative fiat, but such laws do increase unemployment and force people out of free markets into black markets, by forbidding those with low marginal value products (typically the low-skilled, the uneducated, and the young) from offering their services at prices that would command buyers.[193]

Societies characterized by fully equal rights and freedoms will still display income inequalities, just as do unfree societies. (No social order eliminates differences of income; they usually merely disguise the inequalities, as Mancur Olson argued in his essay "The Theory of Soviet-Type Autocracies.")[194] What distinguishes free societies is a general circulation of elites—artistic, cultural, political, and economic. In his general study of the "circulation of elites" among different types of social orders, Vilfredo Pareto noted that, like militant societies, liberal, industrial societies are also characterized by the circulation of elites, but on the basis of entirely different processes. In a militaristic ("bellicose") society, war provides the impetus for "the ordinary soldier to become a general," but in "commercial and industrial societies," for the poorest to attain wealth requires both freedom and "commercial and industrial development of sufficient scale to make this a real possibility for an appreciable number of citizens."[195] Commercial relations based on production and voluntary exchange tend to produce systems of dynamic inequalities, rather than rigidly maintained systems of inequality; that is, persons and families rise and fall in the relative scale of wealth, as the aggregate wealth of the whole society is increasing.[196]

The key distinction that classical liberal sociologists and economists have drawn on in analyzing the ever-changing "distribution of wealth" in free society is that between "ownership," a legal concept, and "wealth," an economic concept. Voluntary exchange entails reallocation not only of ownership rights but of wealth as well, and not only among those who are contractual parties to the exchange. When Henry Ford bought steel, rubber, and glass from vendors and employed workers to make automobiles, he not only caused property to change hands among those involved directly in the exchange but also bid up the value of those resources, caused the value of the resources employed in making horse saddles to go down, and increased the wages of labor by increasing its marginal value product. The transfers of wealth involved were far greater than the value of the property that changed hands in the transactions. Changes in valuation determine what an asset is worth, that is, what wealth it represents for the owner, and values change regularly, as new production processes are introduced, tastes change, and so on, causing the wealth of some to rise and that of others to fall.

> The market economy is thus seen to be a leveling process. In a market economy a process of redistribution of wealth is taking place all the time before which those outwardly similar processes which modern politicians are in the habit of instituting, pale into comparative insignificance, if for no other reason than that the market gives wealth to those who can hold it, while politicians give it to their constituents, who, as a rule, cannot.[197]

Classical liberals have rejected the "natural resource" theory of wealth in favor of an industrial approach. Wealth is not so much what we find, as what we produce. Thus, the influential classical liberal economist Jean-Baptiste Say distinguished "existing materials" (what would today be called "natural resources") from "wealth": "All that man can do is, to re-produce existing materials under another form, which may give them a utility they did not before possess, or merely enlarge one they may have before presented. So that, in fact, there is a creation, not of matter, but of utility; and this I call production of wealth."[198]

There are many societies surrounded by abundant natural resources whose populations are far, far poorer than societies with far fewer resources but governed by institutions that facilitate the creation of wealth. It is a commonplace of development economics, dating back hundreds of years, that abundant resources are not a significant determinant of wealth.[199] Classical liberalism is characterized by the belief that the production of wealth is fostered, and absolute poverty eliminated, by the legal institutions of well-defined and legally secure rights that can be freely exchanged on the basis of a system of contract and law, or Adam Smith's "peace, easy taxes, and a tolerable administration of justice."[200] Moreover, freedom of production and exchange undermined hierarchies, castes, and other rigid forms of inequality.

But wealth production through free markets was never the only classical liberal response to poverty. Such exchanges are but one element in a wider array of cooperative activities to combat poverty.

Self-Help, Mutual Aid, Charity, and Public Assistance

Legal equality is a defining element of the classical liberal tradition, and classical liberals were pioneers in the extension of ideas of equality to both genders, and all races, nations, and social groups. Advocacy of equal rights for women to participate in the workplace, without gender-based job exclusion laws, and to acquire, own, and dispose of property independently has been promoted not only for reasons of moral consistency but to improve the lot of women and eliminate their involuntary dependence on men. As the nineteenth-century classical liberal abolitionist and feminist Sarah Grimké noted, "There are few things which present greater obstacles to the improvement and elevation of woman to her appropriate sphere of usefulness and duty, than the laws which have been enacted to destroy her independence, and crush her individuality; laws which, although they are framed for her government, she has had no voice in establishing, and which rob her of some of her *essential rights*."[201]

The freedom to exercise one's talents led to the improvement of the lot of the oppressed, of the have-nots, of the disadvantaged, of the poor. Self-help was promoted by the elimination of obstacles to self-help and the active assertion of personal responsibility.

But other means were also available. The first, which is widely associated with classical liberalism, is the advocacy of charity as a means to the improvement of the lot of the poor. Charity assists those who have fallen on hard luck or who need assistance from others, which is best provided by voluntary associations. The key for classical liberals was to avoid conditions of permanent dependence. Thus, Bernard Bosanquet, a stalwart of the Charity Organisation Society in Great Britain, was deeply critical of the institutionalization of poverty, of seeing "the institution of 'the poor' as a class, representing, as an ethical idea in the modern mind, a permanent object of compassion and self-sacrifice. 'Poverty,' it has been said, 'has become a status.' The 'déclassés' have become a social class, with the passive social function of stimulating the goodness of others."[202] The purpose of charity was not to further dependency but to foster the ability of the recipients of charity to take care of themselves and their families. Bosanquet argued that economic socialism, based on commands and central planning, would produce selfishness, while voluntary cooperation would produce respect for others and fellow feeling. The experience of life under real existing socialism would seem to have borne out that prediction.[203] And even in the case of modern welfare states, as Norman Barry notes, "Contemporary experience indicates that, far from encouraging a communitarian and socially concerned 'self,' the institutions of the welfare state have simply reproduced the traditional *homo economicus* in a different context."[204]

After self-help, which was promoted primarily by removing obstacles to the free exercise of one's faculties, classical liberals actively promoted and took part in a variety of "friendly societies," "fraternal societies," and "mutual-aid societies" that pooled both the efforts and the risks faced by persons of limited means. At their height, friendly societies actively involved millions of people in social movements that dwarfed the now much-better-known trade-union movements of the time. Although some of them had roots dating back even to the burial societies of ancient Rome, they flourished as never before in the eighteenth, nineteenth, and early to mid-twentieth centuries. As Otto von Gierke observed in 1868 of the "laws of fellowship": "In our century, initiative and creative power have passed back to the people: the free personal fellowship, never entirely extinguished, has been developed into a great number of different branches, and given a form capable of fitting the most varied purposes."[205]

Such fellowships not only provided insurance against illness, accident, death, and other catastrophes but also promoted good character and such virtues as civility, respect for women (male members who beat their wives were normally expelled from societies), sobriety, and charity. Through voluntary association, they went beyond the personal responsibility often associated with classical liberalism and voluntarily embraced various forms of collective responsibility, forms of interaction that are generally underappreciated parts of the classical liberal understanding of liberty and social order. David Schmidtz has argued that "it is internalized responsibility (rather than individual responsibility *per se*) that makes people better off. Institutions that lead people to take responsibility for themselves as a group also help to internalize responsibility, albeit in a collective form. They too can make people better off."[206] Mutual aid was historically a key element in the classical liberal approach to social order and improvement. Like marriage, such associations are seen by classical liberals not as restrictions on liberty, but as exercises of them.

The friendly societies represent perhaps the most poorly documented great social movements ever. (See the essays by David Green and David Beito in this book.) They flourished in many countries as the obstacles to civil association were lowered or eliminated, and they faded away as for-profit firms competed with them by offering actuarially sound insurance policies (in fact, some friendly societies transformed themselves into insurance firms, such as the Modern Woodmen of America, Prudential Insurance, and Metropolitan Life)[207] and as the welfare state displaced them.[208]

Working-class people themselves drew distinctions between the deserving poor and the undeserving poor. Rather than acknowledging any unconditional right to assistance, groups of the poor who pooled their resources for mutual aid distinguished between those who deserved assistance and those who did not, either because of their own unwillingness to assist others when they could or because their situation was of their own voluntary making.

Classical liberal thinkers, as well as the leaders of voluntary organizations, focused on fostering the traits of character suitable for success in civil society. In Green's words, the members of friendly societies "were united not by their physical proximity but by their attachment to shared ideals. Central to the purpose of the societies was the promotion of good character, a consideration of great importance for classical-liberal thought, some of whose advocates tend to take good conduct and a desire for a better life for granted."[209] Assistance from a friendly society was, indeed, a matter of right, but not an unearned or unconditional right.

Mutual aid allowed the poor to escape the paternal condescension that accompanied charity, which was normally associated with cases of extreme desperation. Being needy was a state that one should seek to avoid, not to embrace.

Charity remains closely connected with classical liberal thought, but it was normally third in the list of methods of helping the poor, after self-help and mutual aid. Transfer payments from taxpayers were considered the least desirable means, to be employed only when other forms of improvement in the lot of the poor were unavailable or inadequate. As John Stuart Mill, in his essay on "The Claims of Labour," noted:

> To give money in alms has never been, either in this country or in most others, a rare virtue. Charitable institutions, and subscriptions for relief of the destitute, already abounded; and if new forms of suffering, or classes of sufferers previously overlooked, were brought to notice, nothing was more natural than to do for them what had already been done for others.[210]

The giving of alms was long associated with sacred obligations and, unsurprisingly, often organized by religious institutions. The giving of alms to the needy has generally been understood in the classical liberal tradition as an exercise of the virtues of generosity and compassion.[211] Thus, classical liberals typically recognized a moral obligation to assist those in need as a result of misfortune and promoted a wide variety of voluntary arrangements to provide such assistance. While voluntary assistance was laudatory and virtuous, compulsion was not. A representative view can be found in Adam Smith's *The Theory of Moral Sentiments*. Although the sentiment of beneficence was a necessary element in virtuous activity ("No action can properly be called virtuous which is not accompanied with the sentiment of self-approbation"),[212] beneficence and charity were trumped by considerations of justice: he noted that "we feel ourselves to be under a stricter obligation to act according to justice, than agreeably to friendship, charity, or generosity: that the practice of these last mentioned virtues seems to be left in some measure of our own choice, but that somehow or other, we feel ourselves to be in a peculiar manner tied, bound and obliged to the observation of justice."[213] According to Smith, in a passage that represented one of the central moral commitments of most later classical liberals, "We must always, however, carefully distinguish what is only blamable, or the proper object of disapprobation, from what force may be employed either to punish or to prevent."[214]

The later utilitarian argument that a redistribution of wealth from the richer to the poorer would merely take what was of little value to the former to give what was of greater value to the latter was solidly rejected by classical liberals, who saw in the idea a threat to the general rules on which free and prosperous societies rest.[215] Thus, in Smith's words, "One individual must never prefer himself so much even to any other individual, as to hurt or injure that other, in order to benefit himself, though the benefit to the one should be much greater than the hurt or injury to the other. The poor man must neither defraud nor steal from the rich, though the acquisition might be much more beneficial to the one than the loss could be hurtful to the other." To do so would violate "one of those sacred rules, upon the tolerable observation of which depend the whole security and peace of human society."[216]

Bertrand de Jouvenel addressed directly the utilitarian arguments for redistribution: a leveling of income or wealth to maximize welfare (small reductions in the welfare of the rich being much more than offset by large improvements in the welfare of the poor) would effectively eliminate the expenditures on higher culture associated with wealth, which the advocates of redistribution invariably address by calling for taxation to redirect resources toward support of cultural establishments. As de Jouvenel noted, "All advocates of extreme redistribution couple it with most generous measures of state support for the whole superstructure of cultural activities."[217] He accused them of inconsistency, for the utilitarian welfare-maximization argument for income redistribution was undercut by the redirection of wealth by the state to favored cultural institutions: "It is then an inconsistency, and a very blatant one, to intervene with state support for such cultural activities as do not find a market. Those who spontaneously correct their schemes of redistribution by schemes for such support are in fact denying that the ideal allocation of resources and activities is that which maximizes the sum of satisfactions."[218]

J. S. Mill noted that the imposition of a "moral or a legal obligation, upon the higher classes, that they shall be answerable for the well-doing and well-being of the lower," was characteristic not of liberal societies but of illiberal societies. As he argued, "the ideal state of society which the new philanthropists [advocates of compulsory assistance] are contending for" was that of "the Russian boors." He continued, "There are other labourers, not merely tillers of the soil, but workers in great establishments partaking of the nature of manufactories, for whom the laws of our own country, even in our own time, compelled their employers to find wholesome food, and sufficient lodging and clothing. Who are these? The slaves on a West Indian estate."[219]

Compulsory assistance was associated in the minds of classical liberals not only with condescension but with systems of paternalistic control and loss of independence and liberty. The experience of the Poor Laws and the associated controls of behavior were still vivid memories for the liberals of the nineteenth and twentieth centuries. As Mill noted, "There are governments in Europe who look upon it as part of their duty to take care of the physical well-being and comfort of the people . . . But with paternal care is connected paternal authority. In these states we find severe restrictions on marriage. No one is permitted to marry, unless he satisfies the authorities that he has a rational prospect of being able to support a family."[220]

The fear of such controls has motivated much classical liberal opposition to, or at least uneasiness with, "welfare reform" schemes that require labor for the state as a condition for receipt of assistance.

A major concern about compulsory redistribution that was central to the critique of the Poor Laws and continues to this day in debates on welfare policy and "foreign aid" is whether such state measures actually improve the well-being of the poor, or merely make those who advocate them feel good about themselves, as if they had discharged a moral obligation, not by helping others but by advocating policies. For most classical liberals, consequences, and not merely stated intentions, matter in the evaluation of policies.[221] Thus, the question of whether state aid resting on compulsion in fact represents an improvement for the poor has always been a central concern of classical liberals when addressing plans of redistribution.

In listing the order of preferences among classical liberals, Wilhelm Röpke stated that "our rule and norm and our cheerfully accepted ideal should be security through individual effort and responsibility, supplemented by mutual aid."[222] Röpke differed from some classical liberals in accepting state provision of a minimum of assistance:

> We cannot, nowadays, do without a certain minimum of compulsory state institutions for social security. Public old-age pensions, health insurance, accident insurance, widows' benefits, unemployment relief—there must naturally be room for all these in our concept of a sound social security system in a free society, however little enthusiasm we may feel for them. It is not their principle which is in question, but their extent, organization, and spirit.[223]

Many classical liberals have thus accepted some state provision, but only with some reluctance and as the least preferred method of assistance to the poor. Milton Friedman, for example, offered two reasons to support a limited degree of state compulsion for purposes of assisting the poor. The first was the exercise of legal compulsion to force people to purchase annuities for their own old age because "the improvident will not suffer the consequences of their own action but will impose costs on others. We shall not, it is said, be willing to see the indigent aged suffer in dire poverty. We shall assist them by private and public charity. Hence the man who does not provide for his old age will become a public charge. Compelling him to buy an annuity is justified not for his own good but for the good of the rest of us."[224] (As he quickly noted, "The weight of this argument clearly depends on fact.") The second was the exercise of legal compulsion to force taxpayers as a class to support those who are in need, on the grounds that state coercion to provide a collective (or public) good is acceptable on liberal grounds: "It can be argued that private charity is insufficient because the benefits from it accrue to people other than those who make the gifts. . . . I am distressed by the sight of poverty; I am benefited by its alleviation; but I am benefited equally whether I or someone else pays for its alleviation; the benefits of other people's charity therefore partly accrue to me." Such concerns would, according to Friedman, set "a floor under the standard of life of every person in the community."[225]

F. A. Hayek, although not an enthusiast for the welfare state, also argued, on the grounds of provision of public goods, that some limited state provision of welfare was compatible with classical liberal principles: "All modern governments have made provision for the indigent, unfortunate, and disabled and have concerned themselves with questions of health and the dissemination of knowledge. There is no reason why the volume of these pure service activities should not increase with the general growth of wealth. There are common needs that can be satisfied only by collective action and which can be thus provided for without restricting individual liberty."[226]

Friedman's and Hayek's public goods argument was rejected by Robert Nozick, who offered a more consistently antistatist interpretation of classical liberalism. After a discussion of the economics and the ethics of public goods, Nozick concluded, "Since it would violate moral constraints to compel people who are entitled to their holdings to contribute against their will, proponents of such compulsion should attempt to persuade people to ignore the relatively few who don't go along with the scheme of voluntary contributions. Or, is it relatively *many* who are to be compelled to contribute, though they would not so choose, by those who don't want to feel they are 'suckers'?"[227]

The debates among classical liberals on those issues have been vigorous and have focused on a number of questions, such as how competent and trustworthy state institutions—even subject to democratic supervision—may be, whether any compulsion at all is consistent with the principles of liberalism, and whether state provision of even a "safety net" would set in motion a process of fostering dependence and displacing the network of mutual-aid associations that was closely associated with classical liberalism.

The legal theorist A. V. Dicey expressed the fear of state provision that was general among classical liberals:

> The beneficial effect of State intervention, especially in the form of legislation, is direct, immediate, and, so to speak, visible, whilst its evil effects are gradual and indirect, and lie out of sight . . . . few are those who realize the undeniable truth that State help kills self-help. Hence the majority of mankind must almost of necessity look with undue favour upon governmental intervention. This natural bias can be counteracted only by the existence, in a given society, as in England between 1830 and 1860, of a presumption or prejudice in favour of individual liberty—that is, of *laissez faire*. The mere decline, therefore, of faith in self-help—and that such a decline has taken place is certain—is of itself sufficient to account for the growth of legislation tending towards socialism.[228]

Herbert Spencer, toward the end of his life, saw the growth of the state provision of services and of measures to substitute coercion for voluntary action as "the New Toryism" and "the

Coming Slavery."[229] Like other classical liberals toward the end of the nineteenth century, he connected the rise of nationalism, imperialism, racism, socialism, and the welfare state as outgrowths from the shared root of collectivism.[230]

The fear of state provision was not limited to Anglo-Saxons but was—and remains—a common feature of classical liberal thought. As François Guizot noted, "Nothing is more evident or sacred than the duty of the government to come to the assistance of the classes less favoured by fate, to ease their wretchedness and to assist them in their endeavour to rise toward the blessings of civilization. But to maintain that it is through the defects in the social organisation that all the misery of so many human beings originates, and to impose on the government the task of guaranteeing and distributing equally the good things of life, is to ignore absolutely the human condition, abolish the responsibility inherent in human liberty and excite bad passions through false hopes."[231] Wilhelm von Humboldt despised the Poor Laws for killing charity and hardening hearts: "Does anything tend so effectually to deaden and destroy all true sympathy—all hopeful yet modest entreaty—all trust in man by man? Does not everyone despise the beggar, who finds it more convenient to be cared for in an almshouse than, after struggling with want, to find, not a mere hand flinging him a pittance, but a sympathizing heart?"[232]

There remain questions of the extent of moral obligations to the poor. Those are not easily answered from within the classical liberal tradition, for the simple reason that classical liberal thought distinguishes—as many other traditions do not—between those duties and obligations that are enforceable and those that are not. A classical liberal may embrace the obligation of tithing or of *zakat* but will insist that that obligation may not be made compulsory; it is an expression of one's religious and moral—not legal—obligations. The universalist tendencies of classical liberalism have generally promoted concerns with persons *per se* rather than with co-religionists or co-nationals. The responsibility of not harming others is applicable to all, regardless of whether they are close members of one's own community or complete strangers living in a far-distant nation. As Adam Smith noted, "Mere justice is, upon most occasions, but a negative virtue, and only hinders us from hurting our neighbour. The man who barely abstains from violating either the person, or the estate, or the reputation of his neighbours, has surely very little positive merit. He fulfils, however, all the rules of what is peculiarly called justice, and does every thing which his equals can with propriety force him to do, or which they can punish him for not doing. We may often fulfil all the rules of justice by sitting still and doing nothing."[233] Positive obligations, in the classical liberal view, are normally acquired on the basis of one's acts (they are adventitious rather than connate);[234] as such, one is not born with or assigned particular enforceable obligations to particular people on the basis of the relative poverty of those persons. Because of their focus on eliminating injustice, in the form of the harms visited by some on others, classical liberals led the international movements to abolish forced labor[235] and slavery, which movements promoted the freedom and well-being of the worst-off and most abused members of humanity. Similarly, the moral urgency of the classical liberal case for freedom of trade has focused a substantial amount of attention on the denial of opportunities for improved welfare among the people of poor nations, who are sacrificed by protectionist policies to the well-being of those much wealthier than they. Freeing the poor from coercive controls over their behavior benefits the poor, as well as all who engage in trade; classical liberals see the gains from trade as mutual. It is not a concession to others to remove restrictions on one's own ability to purchase freely. As the nineteenth-century German classical liberal economist and parliamentarian John Prince Smith argued, "The removal of import tariffs is an economic concession which we grant primarily to ourselves and not merely to foreign countries."[236]

The same logic has been applied to immigration, as classical liberals have generally promoted freedom of movement as much as they have freedom of trade.[237] As such, classical liberals have been active proponents of "globalization" through freedom of speech, trade, and travel.[238] It is ironic that socialists and welfare statists often pose as champions of the poor at the same time that they vigorously defend restrictions on migration that use barbed wire, armed patrols, and other forms of force to keep desperately poor people away from wealthy countries where they would have opportunities to improve their lot. Classical liberals have traditionally opposed such restrictions and favor freedom of trade, travel, and migration, which they consider a superior alternative to state redistributive programs that, they generally argue, are unsuccessful at lifting people from poverty to wealth.

Classical liberal thinkers, despite often robust disagreement among themselves, have agreed that the creation of more wealth is the solution to the alleviation of poverty and that, because outcomes are not themselves generally subject to choice, just and efficient institutions are the key to increasing wealth and diminishing poverty. Moreover, although many make room for state provision of assistance to the poor and indigent, all agree that there is a hierarchy of means for the alleviation of poverty, cascading from personal responsibility and self-help, to mutual aid, to charity, to the least preferred option, state compulsion.

A Little Further Reading for Fun and Understanding (and Better School Papers)

Like cancerous tumors, welfare states continue to metastasize, to grow in size, and to threaten the health of the societies from which they draw their sustenance. Like any threat to society, they deserve additional study. In this volume, many additional books and articles are cited in endnotes, and students of the welfare state may wish to consult some of them. There is a great deal of literature defending the welfare state and a student of the welfare state should examine the issue from various perspectives. The first book listed below, Prof. Norman Barry's Welfare, *offers a good overview of issues and a guide to the literature on all sides. The other books listed focus on offering criticisms and alternatives to the welfare state.*

—*Tom G. Palmer*

Welfare, by Norman Barry (Buckingham, UK: Open University Press, 1990). This short book provides an even-handed overview of the history, functioning, and justifications and criticisms of the welfare state.

From Mutual Aid to the Welfare State: Fraternal Societies and Social Services, 1890–1967, by David Beito (Chapel Hill, NC: University of North Carolina, 2000). Historian David Beito documents and describes the history in the US of mutual-aid societies, which provided solidarity, welfare, and uplift to millions of people, but were systematically displaced by welfare state policies throughout the twentieth century.

Reinventing Civil Society: The Rediscovery of Welfare without Politics, by David Green (London: Civitas, 1993). Historian and political scientist David Green has pioneered the study of "friendly societies" in British and Australian society. Not only does Green document the history and explain the benefits of friendly societies, but he puts them in the context of the general classical liberal understanding of civil society. (This book can be downloaded at www.civitas.org.uk/pdf/cw17.pdf.)

The Ethics of Redistribution, by Bertrand de Jouvenel (Indianapolis: Liberty Fund, 1990). This short book is based on lectures by the famous French political scientist that he delivered at Cambridge University. It offers a powerful critical examination of the arguments made for redistribution of income.

A Life of One's Own: Individual Rights and the Welfare State, by David Kelley (Washington, DC: Cato Institute, 1998). A moral philosopher examines the philosophical foundations of the welfare state and subjects them to criticism from a classical liberal perspective.

Realizing Freedom: Libertarian Theory, History, and Practice, by Tom G. Palmer (Washington, DC: Cato Institute, 2009). This collection of essays by the editor of *After the Welfare State* contains several criticisms of the theory of "welfare rights," including the essay "Saving Rights Theory from Its Friends" (originally published in *Individual Rights Reconsidered,* edited by Tibor Machan [Stanford: Hoover Institution Press, 2001], available online at tomgpalmer.com/wp-content/uploads/papers/palmer-individualrightsreconsidered-chapter2.pdf).

The Swedish Model Reassessed: Affluence Despite the Welfare State, by Nima Sanandaji (Helsinki: Libera Institute, 2011). This short study of the Swedish welfare state offers comparative insights on the sources of prosperity in Sweden and the impact of the welfare state there. (It is available online at www.libera.fi/wp-content/uploads/2011/10/Libera_The-Swedish-model.pdf.)

Is the Welfare State Justified?, by Daniel Shapiro (Cambridge: Cambridge University Press, 2007). This book describes commonly advanced justifications for institutions and practices, looks at evidence of how welfare state institutions actually function, and then asks whether the institutions of the welfare state are justified according to the most commonly held substantive views of justice. This book is an academic work in moral philosophy that is nonetheless very readable and accessible.

Editor's note: Contributors to this volume give several slightly different figures for the present value of governmental budgetary imbalances. The differences reflect differing estimates of future conditions, different categories of programs, and different time horizons over which the numbers are calculated. Regardless of such differences, all of the calculations arrive at staggering sums that dwarf officially acknowledged government debt. The unfunded liabilities of modern welfare states are enormous and present very serious threats to the well-being of those who are young today. They reflect the gross irresponsibility of their elders, who allowed this to happen.

Dr. Tom G. Palmer is executive vice president for international programs at the Atlas Network. He oversees the work of teams working around the world to advance the principles of classical liberalism and works with a global network of think tanks and research institutes. Dr. Palmer is a senior fellow of the Cato Institute, where he was formerly vice president for international programs and director of the Center for the Promotion of Human Rights. He was an H. B. Earhart Fellow at Hertford College, Oxford University, and a vice president of the Institute for Humane Studies at George Mason University. He is a member of the board of advisors of Students For Liberty. He has published reviews and articles on politics and morality in scholarly journals such as the *Harvard Journal of Law and Public Policy*, *Ethics*, *Critical Review*, and *Constitutional Political Economy*, as well as in publications such as *Slate*, the *Wall Street Journal*, the *New York Times*, *Die Welt*, *Al Hayat*, *Caixing*, the *Washington Post*, and *The Spectator* of London. He received his B.A. in liberal arts from St. Johns College in Annapolis, Maryland; his M.A. in philosophy from The Catholic University of America, Washington, DC; and his doctorate in politics from Oxford University. His scholarship has been published in books from Princeton University Press, Cambridge University Press, Routledge, and other academic publishers, and he is the author of *Realizing Freedom: Libertarian Theory, History, and Practice*, published in 2009 and the editor of *The Morality of Capitalism*, published in 2011.

Endnotes

1   "If land is not owned by anybody, although legal formalism may call it public property, it is used without any regard to the disadvantages resulting. Those who are in a position to appropriate to themselves the returns—lumber and game of the forests, fish of the water areas, and mineral deposits of the subsoil—do not bother about the later effects of their mode of exploitation. For them, erosion of the soil, depletion of the exhaustible resources and other impairments of the future utilization are external costs not entering into their calculation of input and output. They cut down trees without any regard for fresh shoots or reforestation. In hunting and fishing, they do not shrink from methods preventing the repopulation of the hunting and fishing grounds." Ludwig von Mises, *Human Action: A Treatise on Economics,* in 4 vols., ed. Bettina Bien Greaves (Indianapolis: Liberty Fund, 2007). *Vol. 2. Chapter: 6: The Limits of Property Rights and the Problems of External Costs and External Economies.* Accessed from oll.libertyfund.org/title/1894/110599 on 2012-03-25

2   Frédéric Bastiat, *Selected Essays on Political Economy*, trans. Seymour Cain, ed. George B. de Huszar, introduction by F. A. Hayek (Irvington-on-Hudson: Foundation for Economic Education, 1995). Chapter 5: *The State* 1. Accessed from oll. libertyfund.org/title/956/35453 on 2012-04-02

3   "Social Security trust fund sits in West Virginia file cabinet," *USA Today*, February 28, 2005, www.usatoday.com/news/ washington/2005-02-28-trust-fund_x.htm.

4   Ayn Rand, *Atlas Shrugged* (New York: Signet, 1985), pp. 381–82.

5   Many of the claims about immigrants are factually incorrect, as immigrants in the US, at least, typically pay more to the welfare state in taxes than they receive in benefits and in the past have contributed enormously to the economic dynamism and prosperity of the societies to which they emigrated by creating new businesses. The issues are canvassed in chapter three of Jason L. Riley, *Let Them In: The Case for Open Borders* (New York: Gotham Books, 2008), pp. 91–125.

6   The international reach of the welfare state has also had horrendous consequences, which are well documented in a number of studies, including Dambisa Moyo, *Dead Aid: Why Aid Is Not*

Working and How There Is Another Way for Africa (London: Allen Lane, 2009); Graham Hancock, *Lords of Poverty: The Power, Prestige, and Corruption of the International Aid Business* (New York: Atlantic Monthly Press, 1989); and Michael Maren, *The Road to Hell: The Devastating Effects of Foreign Aid and International Charity* (New York: The Free Press, 1997), among many important works. A pioneering study of the effects of aid was P. T. Bauer's Dis*sent on Development* (Cambridge, MA: Harvard University Press, 1976).

7   See the debate on the responsibility and state power in David Schmidtz and Robert E. Goodin, *Social Welfare and Individual Responsibility: For and Against* (Cambridge: Cambridge University Press, 1998).

8   Gretchen Morgenson and Joshua Rosner, *Reckless Endangerment: How Outsized Ambition, Greed, and Corruption Led to Economic Armageddon* (New York: Times Books, Henry Holt & Co., 2011), pp. 2–3.

9   Lew Sichelman, "Bush to Offer Zero Down FHA Loan," *Realty Times*, January 20, 2004, http://realtytimes.com/rt-pages/20040120_zerodown.htm.

10   Gretchen Morgenson and Joshua Rosner, *Reckless Endangerment*, p. 38.

11   "Any mortgage that a GSE [Government Sponsored Enterprise] would securitize was, under the Basel rules [the global regulations adopted by governments], profitable for American banks to originate—and profitable for them to buy back as part of a security." Jeffrey Friedman, "A Crisis of Politics, Not Economics: Complexity, Ignorance, and Policy Failure," *Critical Review*, Vol. 21, Nos. 2–3 (2009), pp. 127–183, p. 144.

12   For more of the details on the combination of Federal Reserve policies to lower interest rates, government-backed "securitization" of mortgages, and international financial regulations that rated government debt and mortgage-backed security as "low risk," see Johan Norberg, *Financial Fiasco: How America's Infatuation with Home Ownership and Easy Money Created the Economic Crisis* (Washington, DC: Cato Institute, 2009). See also *Critical Review*, "Special Issue: Causes of the Crisis," ed. by Jeffrey Friedman, Vol. 21, Nos., 2–3 (2009), and Jeffrey Friedman and Wladimir Kraus, *Engineering the Financial Crisis: Systemic Risk and the Failure of Regulation* (Philadelphia: University of Pennsylvania Press, 2011).

13 Jagadeesh Gokhlae and Kent Smetters, "Do the Markets Care About the $2.4 Trillion U.S. Deficit?" *Financial Analysts Journal*, Vol. 63, No. 3, 2007.

14 Personal communication with the author, March 26, 2012.

15 Daniel Shapiro, *Is the Welfare State Justified?* (Cambridge: Cambridge University Press, 2007), p. 5. Shapiro's book offers a fair-minded comparison of the justificatory claims made on behalf of welfare states with the evidence for their performance.

16 An example is the insistence of welfare state champion James P. Sterba that deliberate killing-by-starvation of productive citizens is appropriate to induce them to produce more so that the state can confiscate and redistribute the results of their productive efforts. Sterba argues that the right to welfare is a "negative right" that is consistent with the freedom of all and proposes, on the basis of following his intuitions, to threaten to confiscate the "nonsurplus resources" of productive people, i.e., not only the surplus over what is necessary to survive, but the food needed for physical survival, as well, in order to induce the productive to produce more for the state to redistribute. This professor of philosophy believes that it is consistent with respecting the freedom of productive people to threaten them with deliberate starvation, for "our producer could respond by doing nothing. The poor [*in practice, of course, the state, allegedly acting on behalf of the poor —TGP*] could then appropriate the nonsurplus resources of the producer, and then, by not producing more, the producer would just waste away, because she is unwilling to be more productive." "Just waste away" is Sterba's euphemism for the catabolysis, edema, organ failure, and other symptoms of death by starvation. James P. Sterba, "Equality is compatible with and required by liberty," in Jan Narveson and James P. Sterba, *Are Liberty and Equality Compatible?: For and Against* (Cambridge: Cambridge University Press, 2010), p. 23. For chilling descriptions of how Sterba's proposal worked in practice, see Timothy Snyder, *Bloodlands: Europe Between Hitler and Stalin* (New York: Basic Books, 2010), and Frank Dikötter, *Mao's Great Famine: The History of China's Most Devastating Catastrophe, 1958–1962* (New York: Walker Publishing Co., 2010). Sweeping proposals based purely on intuitions about morality and justice that are untested against any knowledge of economics, sociology, or history generally lead to disaster and are, to say the least, morally irresponsible.

17 There is an abundant literature on the moral claims regarding the welfare state, mostly starting with intentions and ending

with intentions. I address some of that literature in my essay "Saving Rights Theory from Its Friends," which originally appeared in *Individual Rights Reconsidered*, ed. by Tibor Machan (Stanford: Hoover Institution Press, 2001). That version can be downloaded from http://tomgpalmer.com/wp-content/uploads/papers/palmer-individualrightsreconsidered-chapter2.pdf. It was reprinted in Tom G. Palmer, *Realizing Freedom: Libertarian Theory, History, and Practice* (Washington, DC: Cato Institute, 2009), pp. 41–83.

18   They have also generated a great deal of "morals legislation" to direct behavior toward what is considered virtuous by political elites. Those measures have included prohibiting prostitution, sterilizing the "morally degenerate," forbidding intoxicants (including alcohol, marijuana, opiates, etc.), outlawing interracial marriage, persecuting and criminalizing minority sexualities, banning behavior considered too risky to oneself, and generally suppressing substances and behaviors deemed incompatible with the welfare of the people. In recent years, as popular mores have changed, welfare states have sometimes changed with them, but the history of such "progressive" states is one of censoriousness and moralistic repression.

19   Daniel Shapiro makes the point that "government rationing generally favors the knowledgeable, connected, and well-motivated middle class." Daniel Shapiro, *Is the Welfare State Justified?*, p. 149.

20   Quoted in Brink Lindsey, *Against the Dead Hand: The Uncertain Struggle for Global Capitalism* (New York: John Wiley & Sons, 2002), p. 33.

21   A. J. P. Taylor, *Bismarck: The Man and the Statesman* (1955; New York: Sutton Publishing, 2003), p. 204. Taylor points out that one element of Bismarck's plan was defeated in the Reichstag; he wanted an element of the "contribution" to be directly from the state budget. Instead, the Reichstag only imposed a contribution to be paid directly by the employee and another alleged to be paid "by the employer." As economists know, however, one hundred percent of the burden for both "shares" fell on the employee, because it came from money that otherwise would have been paid in wages; employers will pay the value of the work done, and not more, and tend to be indifferent to how much the employee receives in cash. Bismarck was pioneering the idea of a state formed by "corporative associations," which represented group interests, rather than representations of citizens with individual rights. As Taylor notes, "The idea carried

further his emphasis on interest-groups instead of high principle. The phrase and the device were to be picked up again by the twentieth-century exponents of Fascism." (p. 204) The piling of additional taxes on labor in the form of "employer's shares" of social security contributions contributed to the collapse of the parliamentary government of the Weimar Republic, as Jürgen von Kruedener, "Die Überforderungen der Weimarer Republik als Sozialstaat," *Geschichte und Gesellschaft*, 11, no. 3 (1985), pp. 358–76, notes, for the collapse "was the consequence of the overstretched welfarism of the state, to which the wage and the wage burden contributed as a major cause." (p. 376)

22 Quoted in *A. J. P. Taylor, Bismarck: The Man and the Statesman*, p. 203.

23 Speech of May 18, 1889, quoted in David Kelley, *A Life of One's Own: Individual Rights and the Welfare State* (Washington, DC: Cato Institute, 1998), p. 39.

24 A. J. P. Taylor, *Bismarck: The Man and the Statesman*, p. 203. Taylor notes that Bismarck pioneered a wide range of welfare state schemes, and "At the end he talked of 'the right to work' and thought of insurance against unemployment—the final step to the welfare state of the twentieth century." (p. 204)

25 Jürgen von Kruedener, "Die Überforderungen der Weimarer Republik als Sozialstaat," shows the results of precisely what Bismarck had pioneered; the burden on workers of the so-called "employer's share" of "social security" payments rose dramatically during the Weimar Republic. Kruedener concludes, "The fateful pitfall, indeed the tragedy of this state, was that it was objectively overstretched as a welfare state." (p. 376)

26 Götz Aly, *Hitler's Beneficiaries: Plunder, Racial War, and the Nazi Welfare State* (New York: Henry Holt & Co., 2006), p. 13. Aly describes the plunder of the Jews of Germany, prior to the plundering of the rest of Europe: "By late 1937, civil servants in the Finance Ministry had pushed the state's credit limit as far as it could go. Forced to come up with ever more creative ways of refinancing the national debt, they turned their attention to property owned by German Jews, which was soon confiscated and added to the so-called *Volksvermögen*, or the collective assets of the German people. The ideologically charged concept of collective assets, which was by no means restricted to German society, implied the possibility of dispossessing those considered 'alien' (*Volksfremden*) or 'hostile' (*Volksfeinden*) to the ethnic mainstream." (p. 41) Forced labor, far from a subsidy to big

private firms, was a redistribution from the enslaved Jews, Poles, Ukrainians, and others to the state as a whole. After calculating the taxes levied by the state on "wages" paid by firms to conscripted labor ("60 to 70 percent of the wages paid by those firms"), Aly concludes that it represented from 1941 to 1945 13 billion Reichsmarks (today about $150 billion): "The size of this figure belies the traditional historical assumption that it was companies that profited most from forced labor. Instead, the exploitation was perpetrated on a far grander scale, by the whole of society itself. The billions in state revenues from forced labor took a significant load off ordinary German taxpayers. And this was only one of the advantages that 'ethnic comrades' derived from their acceptance of a government campaign not only to wage war against others but to dispossess them of everything they had." (p. 162–63)

27 Ibid., p. 303.

28 Friedrich Engels, "Outlines of a Critique of Political Economy," in Lawrence S. Stepelevich, ed., *The Young Hegelians: An Anthology* (Amherst, N.Y.: Humanity Books, 1999), pp. 278–302, p. 283.

29 Ibid., p. 289.

30 Ibid., p. 293.

31 See Jerry Z. Muller, "The Long Shadow of Usury: Capitalism and the Jews in Modern European Thought," in his *Capitalism and the Jews* (Princeton: Princeton University Press, 2010), pp. 15–71.

32 Sheri Berman, *The Primacy of Politics: Social Democracy and the Making of Europe's Twentieth Century* (Cambridge: Cambridge University Press, 2006), pp. 13–14.

33 Ibid., pp. 16–17.

34 94 US 126 (1877), quoted in Douglass C. North, Terry L. Anderson, and Peter J. Hill, *Growth & Welfare in the American Past: A New Economic History* (Englewood Cliffs, N.J.: Prentice Hall, 1983), p. 146.

35 Herbert Hoover, "Address Accepting the Republican Presidential Nomination," August 11, 1932, www.presidency.ucsb.edu/ws/index.php?pid=23198&st=&st1=#axzz1rUPyI5Ew. See also Murray N. Rothbard, "Herbert Hoover and the Myth of Laissez-Faire," in Ronald Radosh and Murray N. Rothbard, eds., *A New*

History of Leviathan (New York: E. P. Dutton & Co., 1972), pp. 111–145.

36 Franklin D. Roosevelt, "Campaign Address on Agriculture and Tariffs," *The public papers and addresses of Franklin D. Roosevelt. Volume one, The genesis of the New Deal, 1928–1932* (New York: Random House, 1938), p. 742.

37 See Amity Shlaes, *The Forgotten Man: A New History of the Great Depression* (New York: Harper, 2007), Douglas A. Irwin, *Peddling Protectionism: Smoot-Hawley and the Great Depression* (Princeton: Princeton University Press, 2011), and Gene Smiley, *Rethinking the Great Depression* (Chicago: Ivan R. Dee, 2002).

38 For an examination of the similarities (combined with repeated statements of the clear differences, as well), see John A. Garraty, "The New Deal, National Socialism, and the Great Depression," *The American Historical Review*, Vol. 78, No. 4 (October, 1973), pp. 907–94, and Wolfgang Schivelbusch, *Three New Deals: Reflections on Roosevelt's America, Mussolini's Italy, and Hitler's Germany, 1933–1939* (New York: Henry Holt & Co., 2006). Mussolini, in fact, in 1934 looked quite favorably on the New Deal: "The American experiment should be followed very closely. In the United States, Government intervention in business is direct; and sometimes it takes a preemptory form. The codes are nothing more than collective contracts to which the President compels both parties to submit. We must wait before passing judgment on that experiment." Benito Mussolini, "Speech in the Senate on the Bill Establishing the Corporations," 13th January 1934, in Benito Mussolini, *The Doctrine of Fascism* (Rome: Ardita, 1935; republished New York: Howard Fertig, 2006), p. 69.

39 From Hanes Walton, *Invisible Politics: Black Political Behavior* (Albany: State University of New York Press, 1985), p. 123.

40 Frances Fox Piven, "The Great Society as Political Strategy," in Richard A. Cloward and Frances Fox Piven, *The Politics of Turmoil: Poverty, Race, and the Urban Crisis* (New York: Vintage Books, 1975), pp. 271–83, pp. 271–72.

41 Ibid., pp. 276–77.

42 Ibid., p. 283.

43 http://bls.gov/news.release/youth.t01.htm.

44   Walter E. Williams, *Race and Economics: How Much Can Be Blamed on Discrimination?* (Stanford: Hoover Institution Press, 2011), pp. 41–43.

45   Charles Murray, *Losing Ground: American Social Policy, 1950–1980* (New York: Basic Books, 1984), introduction to 1994 tenth anniversary edition, p. xviii.

46   Daniel P. Moynihan, *The Politics of a Guaranteed Income* (New York: Vintage Books, 1973), p. 54. Economist Walter E. Williams noted in 1980, "It turns out that if we tallied all federal, state, and local annual expenditures that are justified on the basis of fighting some aspect of poverty, we would find that over $250 billion dollars is spent on these programs. It turns out that if we were simply to give that money to the poor, each poor family of four would receive about $40,000 per year. They do not get that money. Most of it goes to non-poor people, bureaucrats, and professionals charged with caring for the poor. It is like feeding the sparrows through the horses." Walter E. Williams, "The Poor as First Victims of the Welfare State," *Imprimis*, Vol. 9, No. 7 (July 1980), p. 6. Williams's book *The State Against Blacks* (New York: McGraw-Hill, 1982) presented a compelling and well-documented indictment of the entire system of interventionism as harmful to those allegedly being helped by the welfare state. Some of the data have been updated in his book *Race and Economics: How Much Can Be Blamed on Discrimination?*

47   Richard A. Cloward and Frances Fox Piven, *The Politics of Turmoil*, p. 4.

48   Walter E. Williams, *Black America and Organized Labor: A Fair Deal?* (Washington, DC: Lincoln Institute for Research and Education, 1980), p. 25.

49   Edward Tufte, *Political Control of the Economy* (Princeton: Princeton University Press, 1978), p. 143.

50   Cited in Testimony of Cato Institute Senior Fellow Jagadeesh Gokhale to the Committee on Homeland Security and Government Affairs, Subcommittee on Federal Financial Management, Government Information, and International Security, 109th Cong., 1st sess., September 22, 2005, www.hsgac. senate.gov/download/092205gokhale. See also Dallas Federal Reserve CEO Richard Fisher, "Storms on the Horizon: Remarks before the Commonwealth Club of California," www.dallasfed. org/news/speeches/fisher/2008/fs080528.cfm.

51 "President's Health 'Reform' Grows Unfunded Obligations By $17 Trillion," http://budget.senate.gov/republican/public/index.cfm/2012/3/president-s-health-reform-grows-unfunded-obligations-by-17-trillion

52 Richard Fisher, "Storms on the Horizon."

53 The trendline test is explained in Charles Murray, *What It Means to Be a Libertarian: A Personal Interpretation* (New York: Broadway Books, 1997), pp. 47–56.

54 Simon Cordery, *British Friendly Societies, 1750–1914* (New York: Palgrave Macmillan, 2003), p. 1.

55 See David Beito, *From Mutual Aid to the Welfare State: Fraternal Societies and Social Services, 1890–1967* (Chapel Hill: University of North Carolina Press, 2000); David Green, *Working Class Patients and the Medical Establishment* (New York: St. Martin's Press, 1985); Nicolas Marques, "Le monopole de la sécurité sociale face à l'histoire des premières protections sociales." *Journal des Économistes et des Études Humaines*, vol. X n° 2, Sept-Oct. 2000, www.euro92.com/acrob/marques%20mutuelles.pdf; David G. Green and Lawrence Cromwell, *Mutual Aid or Welfare State: Australia's Friendly Societies* (Sydney: Allen & Unwin, 1984); David Green, *Reinventing Civil Society: The Rediscovery of Welfare Without Politics* (London: Institute of Economic Affairs, 2000); Anton Howes, "Friendly Societies, the State and the Medical Profession in Great Britain 1900–1939," unpublished thesis, King's College, London, 2012.

56 E. P. Hennock, *The Origin of the Welfare State in England and Germany, 1850–1914* (Cambridge: Cambridge University Press, 2007), p. 176. Hennock seems not to understand (as many did not at the time) that the so-called "employer's contribution" came entirely from the worker's pay packet and did not represent a transfer from employers to employees, but merely a reduction in the employee's take-home pay.

57 Ibid., p. 92.

58 Quoted in James Bartholomew, *The Welfare State We're In* (London: Politico's, 2004), p. 153. Bartholomew's book admirably both shows how the welfare state has been credited for advances that were due to other causes and documents such negative effects of the welfare state as the deterioration of civility and the rise of dependency, criminality, and other pathologies of modern societies. West's books pioneered

the study of education without the state. A short essay on the topic, "The Spread of Education Before Compulsion: Britain and America in the Nineteenth Century," can be found in *The Freeman*, Vol. 46, Issue 7 (July 1996), www.thefreemanonline.org/featured/the-spread-of-education-before-compulsion-britain-and-america-in-the-nineteenth-century/. For a survey of the issues, see James Tooley, *Education Without the State* (London: Institute of Economic Affairs, 1998), esp. chapter 3, "The Secret History of Education Without the State." www.iea.org.uk/sites/default/files/publications/files/upldbook56pdf.pdf.

59   James Tooley, *The Beautiful Tree: A Personal Journal into How the World's Poorest Are Educating Themselves* (Washington, DC: Cato Institute, 2009).

60   *Oddfellows' Magazine*, No. 414 (June 1909), cited in Simon Cordery, *British Friendly Societies, 1750–1914, p. 155.*

61   Herbert Spencer, "The New Toryism" [1884], in Herbert Spencer, *Political Writings*, ed. by John Offer (Cambridge: Cambridge University Press, 1994), p. 69.

62   See also Mark Pennington, *Robust Political Economy: Classical Liberalism and the Future of Public Policy* (Cheltenham: Edward Elgar, 2011) for an expansion of the general point that processes, rather than outcomes, are the normal subject of political choice.

63   Benjamin Constant, "The Liberty of the Ancients Compared with that of the Moderns" [1819], in Benjamin Constant, *Political Writings,* ed. by Biancamaria Fontana (Cambridge: Cambridge University Press, 1988), p. 326.

64   For a comparison with the Australian friendly societies see David G. Green and Lawrence Cromwell, *Mutual Aid or Welfare State*.

65   P. H. J. H. Gosden, *The Friendly Societies in England 1815–1875* (Manchester: Manchester University Press, 1961), pp. 4–5.

66   P. H. J. H. Gosden, *Self-Help* (London: Batsford, 1973), p. 91; William (Lord) Beveridge, *Voluntary Action* (London: Allen & Unwin, 1948), p. 328.

67   P. H. J. H. Gosden, *The Friendly Societies in England*, p. 18.

68   Ancient Order of Foresters, *General Laws*, Observations on the Advantages of Forestry, 1857.

69   Josef Maria Baernreither, *English Associations of Working Men* (London: Swan Sonnenschein, 1893), p. 380; G. D. Langridge,, *A Lecture on the Origin, Rise and Progress of the Manchester Unity Independent Order of Odd Fellows* (Melbourne: Manchester Unity, 1867), pp. 20–21.

70   Sidney and Beatrice Webb, *Industrial Democracy* (London: The Authors, 1913), p. 36, note 1.

71   Ancient Order of Foresters, Lecture 1, 1879, pp. 41–42.

72   Ancient Order of Foresters, Court *Robert Gordon*, Rules 53 and 55, 1877.

73   Ancient Order of Foresters, *Formularies,* 1879, p. 12.

74   Ancient Order of Foresters, *General Laws*, 1857, Rule 82.

75   Independent Order of Oddfellows, Manchester Unity, *Lodge Ritual and Lecture Book with Procedure*, 1976, pp. 9–10.

76   William (Lord) Beveridge, *Voluntary Action*, Table 20.

77   Ibid., Table 22.

78   The estimates for fraternal society membership are from the Report of the President's Research Committee on Social Trends, *Recent Social Trends in the United States,* vol. 2 (New York: McGraw-Hill, 1933), p. 935. The population figures for Americans over twenty are in US Department of Commerce, *Historical Statistics of the United States: Colonial Times to 1970,* pt I (Washington, DC: US Government Printing Office, 1975), pp. 15–20. Fraternal insurance societies accounted for about 10,000,000 of this membership, while secret societies made up the rest. The figures in *Recent Social Trends* work well as rough-and-ready estimates of fraternal membership. A few words of caution, however. By failing to compensate for those individuals who join more than one organization, these figures overestimate fraternal membership. On the other hand, they underestimate membership by not including the members of numerous societies (many of them operated by African Americans and immigrants) and local relief societies organized on neighborhood and occupational levels. While relief societies dispensed mutual aid, they lacked the fraternal attributes of lodge and ritual. For more on relief societies, see Charles Richmond Henderson, *Industrial Insurance in the United States* (Chicago: University of Chicago Press, 1908), pp. 63–83.

79   The best discussion of the ritual's functional role remains Noel P. Gist, "Secret Societies: A Cultural History of Fraternalism," *University of Missouri Studies* 15 (October 1, 1940). Also, see Marc C. Carnes, *Secret Ritual and Manhood in Victorian America* (New Haven, Yale University Press, 1989).

80   Walter Basye, *History and Operation of Fraternal Insurance* (Rochester: the Fraternal Monitor, 1919), pp. 35–36: Lynn Dumenil, *Freemasonry and American Culture, 1880–1930* (Princeton: Princeton University Press, 1984), pp. 225, 22.

81   Lynn Dumenil, *Freemasonry and American Culture, 1880–1930*, p. 21.

82   US Department of Labor, Bureau of Labor Statistics, *Care of Aged Persons in the United States* (Washington, DC: US Government Printing Office, 1929), pp. 162, 15, 163; and Lynn Dumenil, *Freemasonry and American Culture, 1880–1930*, p. 20. In 1929, the bureau identified 112 fraternal homes for the aged in the United States, mostly operated by secret societies for indigent members, housing a population of over 7,000. Several fraternal insurance societies also built such homes, but generally they relied more on insurance to aid their elderly. On fraternal orphanages, see C. W. Areson and H. W. Hopkirk, "Child Welfare Programs of Churches and Fraternal Orders," *The Annals of the American Academy of Political and Social Science 121* (September 1925), pp. 85–95.

83   Harris Dickson and Isidore P. Mantz, "Will the Widow Get Her Money? The Weakness in Fraternal Life Insurance and How It May Be Cured," *Everybody's Magazine 22* (June 1910), p. 776.

84   Este Erwood Buffum, *Modern Woodmen of America: A History*, vol. 2 (Modern Woodmen of America, 1935), p. 5; and Peter Roberts, *Anthracite Coal Communities: A Study of the Demography, the Social, Educational and Moral Life of the Anthracite Regions* (New York: Macmillan, 1904), p. 309.

85   Walter Basye, *History and Operation of Fraternal Insurance*, pp. 15–16: and US Department of Commerce, *Historical Statistics of the United States: Colonial Times to 1970, pt. 1*, p. 168.

86   Illinois Health Insurance Commission, *Report of the Illinois Health Insurance Commission of the State of Illinois* (1919), 224–25.

87   US Department of Labor, *Care of Aged Persons*, 158: and New York Commission on Old-Age Security, *Report of the New York State Commission* (Albany: J. B. Lyons, 1930), pp. 312–13. Cited in Carolyn L. Weaver, *The Crisis in Social Security: Economic and Political Origins* (Durham: Duke University Press, 1982), pp. 41–42. By 1928, about 14 percent of the work force was enrolled in private pension plans. The total number of private pension plans in operation actually increased during the early, and worst, years of the Depression. The common perception – widely propagated both before and after the establishment of Social Security – that the elderly were heavily dependent on poor relief, is a myth. Less than 1 percent of the aged lived in alms houses in 1923, about the same percentage as 1880. Carolyn N. Weaver, *The Crisis in Social Security*, pp. 48, 63.

88   US Department of Labor, Children's Bureau, *Mothers' Aid, 1931* (Washington, DC: US Government Printing Office, 1933), pp. 8, 17; and Michael B. Katz, *In the Shadow of the Poorhouse: A Social History of Welfare in America* (New York: Basic Books, 1980), p. xii. For a good summary of recent literature on the frequency of working class membership in native white fraternal orders, such as the Odd Fellows, Knights of Pythias, and Ancient Order of the United Workmen, see Mary Ann Clawson, *Constructing Brotherhood: Class, Gender, and Fraternalism* (Princeton: Princeton University Press, 1989), 87–110.

89   *Report of the Social Insurance Commission of the State of California* (Sacramento: California State Printing Office, 1917), pp. 81, 89; and *Report of the Illinois Health Insurance Commission of the State of Illinois*, pp. 464. In 1919, the Illinois Health Insurance Commission estimated that 25.8 percent of the wage earners of Chicago had insured (mostly in fraternals) against sickness and 23.7 against disability. Many societies not offering insurance had informal, usually ad hoc, methods to attend to the health problems of members. *Report of the Illinois Health Insurance Commission of the State of Illinois*, pp. 216, 218, 221.

90   *Report of the Social Insurance Commission*, 82, 89, 302: *Report of the Illinois Health Insurance Commission of the State of Illinois*, pp. 123, 474; and Peter Roberts, *Anthracite Coal Communities*, pp. 309–10. In 1929, about 9 percent of industrial employees in the United States lost eight or more work days to illness. US Public Health Service, *Public Health Reports* 47 (January 15, 1932), pp. 136.

91   I am indebted to Jennifer Robach for pointing out possible advantages of fraternal insurance in coping with moral hazard. See her "Social Insurance in Ethnically Diverse Societies," mimeograph, Center for Study of Public Choice, George Mason University, October 1989. For more on early experiments by commercial companies to provide health insurance and the subsequent moral hazard difficulties they encountered, see Frederick L. Hoffman, *History of Prudential Insurance Company of America, 1875–1900* (Prudential Press, 1900), pp. 6–62. In 1909, the prominent insurance executive John F. Dryden, no booster of fraternal societies, claimed that "the assurance of a stipulated sum during sickness can only with safety be transacted and then only in a limited way, by fraternal organizations having a perfect knowledge of and complete supervision over the individual members." John F. Dryden, *Addresses and Papers on Life Insurance and Other Subjects* (Newark: The Prudential Insurance Company of America, 1909), p. 32.

92   *Report of the Social Insurance Commission of the State of California,* p. 110, and Jennifer Roback, "Social Insurance in Ethnically Diverse Societies," p. 10.

93   James G. Burrow, *Organized Medicine in the Progressive Era: The Move Toward Monopoly* (Baltimore: Johns Hopkins University Press, 1977), pp. 121–23.

94   Samuel Silverberg quoted in George Rosen, "Contract or Lodge Practice and its Influence on Medical Attitudes to Health Insurance," *American Journal of Public Health* 67 (April 1977), pp. 374–75.

95   H. T. Partree, "Contract Practice: Its Ethical Bearings and Relations to the Lodge and Industrial Insurance," *Bulletin of the American Academy of Medicine* 10 (December 1909), p. 596; and James G. Burrow, *Organized Medicine in the Progressive Era*, p. 126.

96   George Rosen, "Contract or Lodge Practice and its Influence on Medical Attitudes to Health Insurance," p. 378; and James G. Burrow, *Organized Medicine in the Progressive Era*, pp. 128, 131.

97   Samuel P. Hays, *The Response to Industrialization: 1885–1914* (Chicago: University of Chicago Press, 1957), p. 95.

98   Quoted in Hace Sorel Tishler, *Self-Reliance and Social Security, 1870–1917* (Port Washington: National University Publications,

1971), p. 95. For more on the fraternal (and related mutual aid) societies of selected immigrant groups, see David M. Emmons, *The Butte Irish: Class and Ethnicity in an American Mining Town, 1875–1925* (Urbana: University of Illinois Press, 1989), pp. 94–132: Michael R. Weisser, *A Brotherhood of Memory: Jewish Landsmanshaftn in the New World* (New York: Basic Books, 1985); William I. Thomas, *The Polish Peasant in Europe and America, vol. 2* (New York: Dover Publications, 1958), pp. 1578–1643: and Humbert S. Nelli, *Italians in Chicago, 1880–1930: A Study in Ethnic Mobility* (New York: Oxford University Press, 1970), pp. 156–99.

99   Howard W. Odum, *Social and Mental Traits of the Negro: Research into the Conditions of the Negro Race in Southern Towns* (New York: Columbia University Press, 1910), pp. 102–3, 109, 99.

100   William A. Muraskin, *Middle-class Blacks in a White Society: Prince Hall Freemasonry in America* (Berkeley: University of California Press, 1975), pp. 118, 133–59, 54–56.

101   Booker T. Washington, *The Story of the Negro, The Rise of the Race from Slavery*, vol. 2 (New York: Negro Universities Press, 1969), pp. 148–70; W. E. B. Du Bois, *Economic Cooperation Among Negro Americans* (Atlanta: Atlanta University Press, 1907), pp. 109, 115, 122; and W. E. B. Du Bois, *The Philadelphia Negro: A Social Study* (New York: Schocken Books, 1967), pp. 185–86, 221–27.

      Mexican Americans also formed versions of such "white" societies as the Masons and Woodmen of the World. Most Mexican American fraternal societies (mutualistas), however, did not have direct white parallels. Jose Amaro Hernandez, *Mutual Aid for Survival: The Case of the Mexican American* (Malabar, Florida: Robert E. Krieger Publishing Co., 1983), pp. 65–66.

102   *Report of the Illinois Health Insurance Commission of the State of Illinois*, p. 222.

103   Sadie Tanner Mossell, "The Standard of Living Among One Hundred Negro Migrant Families in Philadelphia," *Annals of the American Academy of Political and Social Science 98* (November 1921), p. 200; Margaret F. Byington, *Homestead: The Households of a Mill Town* (New York: Charities Publication Committee, 1910), p. 91; and Hace Sorel Tishler, *Self-Reliance and Social Security, 1870–1917*, p. 96. This high incidence of African American life insurance policyholding persisted as late as the 1960s. In 1967, the Survey Research Center at the

University of Michigan found that a higher percentage of African Americans than whites held life insurance in every income group. Approximately 80.33 percent of African American families had some life insurance as compared to 77.5 percent of white families. More recent estimates are harder to come by but, in light of the rapid expansion of the welfare state since 1967, it would be fascinating to find out if relative African American and white insurance rates have changed. Cited in Roland W. Bailey, ed., *Black Business Enterprise: Historical and Contemporary Perspectives* (New York; Basic Books, 1971), p. 167.

104   US Department of Labor, Bureau of Labor Statistics, *Monthly Labor Review 28* (March 1929), pp. 421, 424; Charles W. Ferguson, *Fifty Million Brothers: A Panorama of American Lodges and Clubs* (New York: Farrar and Rinehart, 1937), p. 144; and *Report of the Pennsylvania Commission on Old Age Pensions* (Harrisburg, 1919), p. 67.

105   The Hibernians, of course, were Irish Americans. See Michael F. Funchion. ed., *Irish American Voluntary Organizations* (Westport: Greenwood Press, 1938), pp. 51–61.

106   *Fraternal Monitor* 22 (December 1, 1911), p. 16; and *Fraternal Monitor* 19 (January 21, 1908): p. 10–11.

107   Peter Roberts, *Anthracite Coal Communities*, pp. 263–64.

108   Michael B. Katz, *In the Shadow of the Poorhouse,* p. 291; and Katz, *The Undeserving Poor: From the War on Poverty to the War on Welfare* (New York: Pantheon, 1989), pp. 179–80, 184, 239.

109   Mary E. Richmond, *Friendly Visiting among the Poor: A Handbook for Charity Workers* (Montclair, NJ: Patterson Smith 1969), pp. 11–12.

110   On charity organization investigative practices during the early twentieth century, see Walter I. Trattner, *From Poor Law to Welfare State: A History of Social Welfare in America* (New York: Free Press, 1989), pp. 89–92.

111   Michael B. Katz, *The Undeserving Poor,* p. 184; and William A. Muraskin, *Middle Class Blacks in a White Society*, p. 46. Fraternal societies among free African Americans in the North before the Civil War had similar restrictions. In 1832, a group of African Americans observed that in Philadelphia, "the members of these

societies are bound by the rules and regulations, which tend to promote industry and morality among them. For any disregard or violation of these rules for intemperance and immorality of any kind, the members are liable to be suspended or expelled." Leonard P. Curry, *The Free Black in Urban America, 1800–1850: The Shadow of the Dream* (Chicago: University of Chicago Press, 1981), pp. 203–4.

112 William A. Muraskin, *Middle Class Blacks in a White Society*, p. 84–85; and Alan Derickson, *Workers' Health, Workers' Democracy: The Western Miners' Struggle, 1891–1925* (Ithaca: Cornell University Press, 1988), p. 66.

113 I am heavily indebted to Jeffrey Friedman for pointing out the contrast between charity aid and restrictions, based on adversarial relationships, and those of fraternal societies centered around ties of reciprocity.

114 Walter Basye, *History and Operation of Fraternal Insurance*, p. 20; and Michael B. Katz, *The Undeserving Poor*, p. 179. According to Terence O'Donnel, the "*esprit de corps* of a fraternal beneficiary society is one of its most valuable assets, and is far out of proportion to the 'good will' a purely commercial company can claim." Terence O'Donnell, *History of Life Insurance in its Formative Years* (Chicago: American Conservation Company, 1936).

115 *History and Manual of the Colored Knights of Pythias* (Nashville: National Baptist Publishing Board, 1917), pp. 448–49; and Jose Amaro Hernandez, *Mutual Aid for Survival*, p. 93.

116 For an insightful look at some consequences of the decline in mutual aid, see Charles Murray, *In Pursuit: Of Happiness and Good Government* (New York: Simon and Shuster, 1988).

117 William Julius Wilson, *The Truly Disadvantaged: The Inner City, The Underclass, and Public Policy* (Chicago: University of Chicago Press, 1987), p. 3.

118 James Borchert, *Alley Life in Washington: Family, Community, Religion, and Folklore in the City, 1850–1970* (Urbana: University of Illinois Press, 1980), pp. 98, 215–17.

119 I borrowed the topic heading for this section from David G. Green and Lawrence Cromwell, *Mutual Aid or Welfare State: Australia's Friendly Societies*. The friendly societies were the

Australian (as well as British) versions of the American fraternal societies.

120 *Statistics of Fraternal Benefit Societies (1906–86)*. On the decline of the leading secret societies, see Noel P. Gist, "Secret Societies: A Cultural History of Fraternalism," pp. 42–43; Lynn Dumenil, *Freemasonry and American Culture, 1880–1930*, p. 225; and Alvin J. Schmidt and Nicholas Babchuk, "Formal Voluntary Organizations and Change Over Time: A Study of American Fraternal Organizations," *Journal of Action Research 1* (January 1972), p. 49.

121 Gunnar Myrdal, *An American Dilemma: The Negro Problem and Modern Democracy* (New York: Harper and Brothers Publishers, 1944), p: 953; Edward Nelson Palmer, "Negro Secret Societies," *Social Forces 23* (December 1944), p. 211: and William A. Muraskin, *Middle-class Blacks in a White Society*, p. 29.

122 Guy B. Johnson, "Some Factors in the Development of Negro Social Institutions in the United States," *American Journal of Sociology 40* (November 1934), p. 336; and Gunnar Myrdal, *An American Dilemma: The Negro Problem and Modern Democracy*, p. 952. In the last thirty years, a few surveys on voluntary associations have also recorded percentages of fraternal membership. In central Long Beach, California, a 1966 survey found that 14.6 percent of whites belonged to fraternal groups compared to 27.5 percent of African Americans. S. John Dackawich, "Voluntary Associations of Central Area Negroes," *Pacific Sociological Review 9* (Fall 1966), p. 77. In Tampa, Florida in 1967, 8 percent of African Americans belonged to "mutual aid" lodges while 11 percent belonged to "regular" lodges. No percentages for whites were tabulated. Jack C. Ross and Raymond H. Wheeler, *Black Belonging: A Study of the Social Correlates of Work Relations Among Negroes* (Westport: Greenwood Publishing Company, 1971), pp. 106–8. In Austin, Texas in 1969–70, the fraternal membership figure was 16.9 percent for African American males and 13.3 percent for African American females against 10.3 percent for white males and 2 percent for white females. J. Allen Williams, et al., "Voluntary Associations and Minority Status: A Comparative Analysis of Anglo, Black, and Mexican Americans," *American Sociological Review 38* (October 1973), p. 644. In New York City in 1972, fraternal society representation was 7 percent for African American males and 2 percent for African American females, compared to 12 percent for white males and 3 percent for white females. Steven Martin Cohen and Robert E. Kapsis, "Participation of Blacks,

Puerto Ricans, and Whites in Voluntary Associations: A Test of Current Theories," *Social Forces 56* (June 1978), p.1063.

123 Not all scholars agree with Myrdal's interpretation of the African American fraternal society as imitative. See especially Betty M. Kuyk, "The African Derivations of Black Fraternal Orders in the United States," *Comparative Studies in Society and History 25* (October 1983), pp. 559–92. Kuyk cites evidence of heavy borrowing by African American societies of rituals and forms of organization from African American antecedents.

124 John Chodes, "Friendly Societies: Voluntary Social Security and More," *The Freeman 40* (March 1990), p. 98; and Walter Basye, *History and Operation of Fraternal Insurance*, pp. 113–22.

125 Richard De Raismes Kip, *Fraternal Life Insurance in America* (Philadelphia: College Offset Press, 1953), pp. 182–83; and J. Owen Stalson, *Marketing Life Insurance: Its History in America* (Bryn Mawr: McCahan Foundation, 1969), pp. 460–61. A good place to find advertisements for a wide array of societies is any issue of the *Fraternal Monitor*.

126 On the decline of contract practice during the 1920s see John Duffy, *The Healers: The Rise of the Medical Establishment* (New York: McGraw, 1976), pp. 198–99.

127 Roger L. Ransom and Richard Sutch, "Tontine Insurance and the Armstrong Investigation: A Case of Stifled Innovation, 1868–1905," *Journal of Economic History 47* (June 1987), p. 390.

128 Walter I. Trattner, *From Poor Law to Welfare State*, pp. 202–5.

129 For the dampening effect of workers compensation on accident and disability insurance by mutual benefit associations, see US Department of Labor, Bureau of Labor Statistics, *Monthly Labor Review 25* (July 1927), p. 20; *Monthly Labor Review 28* (January 1929), p. 74; and Pierce Williams, *The Purchase of Medical Care Through Fixed Periodic Payment* (New York: National Bureau of Economic Research, 1932), pp. 278–79.

130 Michael B. Katz, *The Undeserving Poor*, pp. 190–91.

131 Herbert G. Gutman, *The Black Family in Slavery and Freedom, 1750–1925* (New York: Pantheon, 1976); Daniel Patrick Moynihan, *The Negro Family: The Case for National Action* (Washington, D.C.: Office of Policy Planning and Research, US Department of Labor, 1965); and William Julius Wilson,

The Truly Disadvantaged, p. 65. In the past decade, other historians, besides Gutman, have uncovered evidence confirming the prevalence of the two-parent African American household in both the North and the South during the late nineteenth and early twentieth centuries. For summaries of the literature, see James Borchert, *Alley Life in Washington*, pp. 57–99; and William Julius Wilson and Kathryn N. Neckerman, "Poverty and Family Structure: The Widening Gap between Evidence and Public Policy Issues," in Sheldon H. Danziger and Daniel H. Weinberg, eds, *Fighting Poverty: What Works and What Doesn't* (Cambridge, Mass.: Harvard University Press, 1986), pp. 232–59.

132   US Department of Commerce, *Historical Statistics of the United States: Colonial Times to 1970, pt. 1,*, p. 15; US Department of Labor, *Mothers' Aid, 1931*, p. 3; *Social Security Bulletin* 53 (August 1990), p. 37; and Nathan Glazer, *The Limits of Social Policy* (Cambridge, Mass.: Harvard University Press, 1988), p. 43. Anthropologist Carol Stack offers immensely useful frame of reference for measuring "the stability and collective power of family life." Stack (whose perspective is similar to that of *Regulating the Poor*) defines the family "as the smallest organized, durable network of kin and non-kin who interact daily, providing domestic needs of children and assuring their survival." Carol B. Stack, *All Our Kin: Strategies for Survival in a Black Community* (New York: Harper and Row, 1974), pp. 31, 90.

133   Piven and Coward not only describe but applaud what they perceive as the greater willingness of today's poor to seek dependence on governmental aid rather than rely on their own resources or accept available job opportunities. Frances Fox Piven, Richard A. Cloward, Barbara Ehrenreich, and Fred Block, *The Mean Season*, pp. 21–22. The current attitudes (at least as related by Piven and Cloward) are quite a contrast to those revealed by James Borchert (see above) in his description of African American and white slum residents of the pre-welfare state era and their strong aversion to charity and poor-relief dependency. A byproduct of replacing reciprocal with dependent relationships has been the decline of the famous "work ethic." The former hegemony of work ethic values among both the poor and the middle class has been noted by a wide variety of historians. See especially Daniel T. Rodgers, *The Work Ethic in Industrial America, 1850–1920* (Chicago: University of Chicago Press, 1978), pp. 168–70. In many ways, the increase acceptance of dependent relationships follows a larger trend among all classes in society (farmers, Savings and Loan executives, etc.).

134 Jo Becker, Sherly Gay Stolberg, and Stephen Labaton, "White House Philosophy Stoked Mortgage Bonfire," *New York Times*, December 21, 2008.

135 G. W. Bush, "President Calls for Expanding Opportunities to Home Ownership: Remarks by the president on homeownership," June 17, 2002, http://georgewbush-whitehouse.archives.gov/news/releases/2002/06/20020617-2.html

136 Jo Becker, Sherly Gay Stolberg, and Stephen Labaton, "White House Philosophy Stoked Mortgage Bonfire," *New York Times*, December 21, 2008.

137 Office of Federal Housing Enterprise Oversight, "Report to Congress," Washington, DC, June 2003, p. 38. The OFHEO used similar language about Fannie Mae on p. 36.

138 Binyamin Appelbaum, Carol D. Leonnig, and David S. Hilzenrath, "How Washington Failed to Rein in Fannie, Freddie," *Washington Post*, September 14, 2008.

139 Peter J. Wallison and Charles Calomiris, "The Last Trillion-Dollar Commitment: The Destruction of Fannie Mae and Freddie Mac," American Enterprise Financial Services Outlook, September 2008.

140 Lisa Lerer, "Fannie, Freddie Spent $200M to Buy Influence," *Politico.com*, July 16, 2008.

141 Charles Duhigg, "Pressured to Take More Risk, Fannie Reached a Tipping Point," *New York Times* October 5, 2008.

142 Binyamin Appelbaum, Carol D. Leonnig, and David S. Hilzenrath, "How Washington Failed to Rein in Fannie, Freddie," *Washington Post*, September 14, 2008.

143 Ibid.

144 Charles Duhigg, "Pressured to Take More Risk, Fannie Reached a Tipping Point," *New York Times* October 5, 2008.

145 Charles Duhigg, "At Freddie Mac, Chief Discarded Warning Signs," *New York Times*, August 5, 2008.

146 Binyamin Appelbaum, Carol D. Leonnig, and David S. Hilzenrath, "How Washington Failed to Rein in Fannie, Freddie," *Washington Post*, September 14, 2008.

147   Paul Krugman, "Fannie, Freddie and You," *New York Times*, July 14, 2008.

148   Seeking Alpha, "Countrywide Financial Q2 2007 Earnings Call Transcript, July 24, 2007," http://seekingalpha.com/article/42171-countrywide-financial-q2-2007-earnings-call-transcript.

149   Carol Leonnig, "How HUD Mortgage Policy Fed the Crisis," *Washington Post,* June 10, 2008.

150   Peter J. Wallison and Charles Calomiris, "The Last Trillion-Dollar Commitment: The Destruction of Fannie Mae and Freddie Mac."

151   Jody Shenn, "Fannie, Freddie Subprime Spree," *Bloomberg. com,* September 22, 2008, www.bloomberg.com/apps/news?pid=20601109&sid=a.6kKtOoO72k&refer=home.

152   James Lockhart, "Reforming the Regulation of the Government Sponsored Enterprises," Statement before the US Senate Banking, Housing, and Urban Affairs Committee, February 7, 2008.

153   Peter J. Wallison and Charles Calomiris, "The Last Trillion-Dollar Commitment: The Destruction of Fannie Mae and Freddie Mac."

154   Nassim Nicholas Taleb, *The Black Swan: The Impact of the Highly Improbable* (London: Penguin Books, 2008), pp. 225–26.

155   Charles Duhigg, "Pressured to Take More Risk, Fannie Reached a Tipping Point," *New York Times* October 5, 2008.

156   John Locke, *Two Treatises of Government,* ed. Peter Laslett (Cambridge: Cambridge University Press, 1988), *Second Treatise,* VI, pp. 57, 306. Note that for Locke the term "property" covers far more than the term does in contemporary English, in which it is limited to what Locke termed "estate." Locke, in contrast, refers to "Lives, Liberties, and Estates, which I call by the general name, *Property.*" Ibid., *Second Treatise,* IX, pp. 123, 350. Compare also James Madison, in his essay "On Property." "This term in its particular application means 'that dominion which one man claims and exercises over the external things of the world, in exclusion of every other individual.' In its larger and juster meaning, it embraces every thing to which a man may attach a value and have a right, and which leaves to every one else the like advantage." *National Gazette,* March 29, 1792, http://press-pubs.uchicago.edu/founders/documents/VIch16823.html.

157 See Anthony de Jasay, "Liberalism, Loose or Strict," *Independent Review* 9, no. 3 (Winter 2005), pp. 427–32.

158 Robert Nozick, *Anarchy, State, and Utopia* (New York: Basic Books, 1974), p. ix.

159 Quoted by Dugald Stewart from a now lost manuscript in Stewart's "Account of the Life and Writings of Adam Smith, LLD," in Adam Smith, *Essays on Philosophical Subject*, ed. W. P. D. Wightman and J. C. Bryce, vol. 3 of the *Glasgow Edition of the Works and Correspondence of Adam Smith* (Indianapolis: Liberty Fund, 1982), p. 322.

160 Nathan Rosenberg and L. E. Birdzell Jr., *How the West Grew Rich: The Economic Transformation of the Industrial World* (New York: Basic Books, 1986), p. 3.

161 Deirdre McCloskey, "1780–1860: A Survey," in *The Economic History of Britain 1700, vol. I: 1700–1860*, ed. Roderick Floud and Deirdre McCloskey (Cambridge: Cambridge University Press, 2000), p. 242.

162 Peter Bauer, *From Subsistence to Exchange* (Princeton, NJ: Princeton University Press, 2000), p. 6.

163 Carlo Cipolla, *Before the Industrial Revolution: European Society and Economy, 1000–1700* (New York: W. W. Norton, 1980), pp. 9–10.

164 Ibid., pp. 18–19. Economic historian Robert William Fogel has placed great stress on the role of access to nutrition in eliminating beggary:
     "The relatively generous poverty program developed in Britain during the second half of the eighteenth century, and the bitter attacks on that program by Malthus and others, have given the unwarranted impression that government transfers played a major role in the secular decline in beggary and homelessness. Despite the relative generosity of English poor relief between 1750 and 1834, beggary and homelessness fluctuated between 10 and 20 percent. Despite the substantial reduction in the proportion of national income transferred to the poor as a result of the poor laws of 1834 and later years, homelessness declined sharply during the late nineteenth century and early twentieth centuries.
     "The fact is that government transfers were incapable of solving the problems of beggary and homelessness during the eighteenth and much of the nineteenth centuries, because the

root cause of the problems was chronic malnutrition. Even during the most generous phase of the relief program, the bottom fifth of the English population was so severely malnourished that it lacked the energy for adequate levels of work.

"At the end of the eighteenth century British agriculture, even when supplemented by imports, was simply not productive enough to provide more than 80 percent of the potential labor force with enough calories to sustain regular manual labor. It was huge increases in English productivity during the later part of the nineteenth and the early twentieth centuries that made it possible to feed even the poor at relatively high caloric levels. Begging and homelessness were reduced to exceedingly low levels, by nineteenth century standards, only when the bottom fifth of the population acquired enough calories to permit regular work."

Robert William Fogel, *The Escape from Hunger and Premature Death, 1700–2100: Europe, America, and the Third World* (Cambridge: Cambridge University Press, 2004), pp. 41–42.

165   F. A. Hayek, *The Fatal Conceit: The Errors of Socialism* (Chicago: University of Chicago Press, 1988), pp. 130–31.

166   The classic refutation can be found in Thomas Babington Macaulay's January 1830 review of Robert Southey's 1829 Tory attack on industrialism, *Sir Thomas More; or, Colloquies on the Progress and Prospects of Society,* in "Southey's Colloquies," in Macaulay, *Critical and Historical Essays, vol. 2* (New York: Dutton, 1967), pp. 187–224. See also for a summary T. S. Ashton, *The Industrial Revolution: 1760–1830* (Oxford: Oxford University Press, 1997).

167   Thomas Babingtom Macaulay, *The History of England from the Accession of James II* (Philadelphia: E. H. Butler, 1849), 291–92. As Macaulay noted in his "Southey's Colloquies," "If we were to prophesy that in the year 1930 a population of fifty millions, better fed, clad, and lodged than the English of our time, will cover these islands, that Sussex and Huntingdonshire will be wealthier than the wealthiest parts of the West Riding of Yorkshire now are, that cultivation, rich as that of a flower-garden, will be carried up to the very tops of Ben Nevis and Helvellyn, that machines constructed on principles yet undiscovered will be in every house, that there will be no highways but railroads, no traveling but by steam, that our debt, vast as it seems to us, will appear to our great-grandchildren a trifling encumbrance, which might easily be paid off in a year or two, many people would think us insane." (p. 223)

168   Étienne Bonnot, Abbé de Condillac, *Commerce and Government Considered in Their Mutual Relationship*, trans. Shelagh Eltis (Cheltenham: Edward Elgar, 1997), p. 103.

169   Adam Smith, *An Inquiry into the Nature and Causes of the Wealth of Nations, vol. 2*, ed. R. H. Campbell and A. S. Skinner (Indianapolis: Liberty Fund, 1981), pp. 869–70.

170   "According therefore, as this produce, or what is purchased with it, bears a greater or smaller proportion to the number of those who are to consume it, the nation will be better or worse supplied with all the necessaries and conveniences for which it has occasion." Adam Smith, *An Inquiry into the Nature and Causes of the Wealth of Nations*, vol. I, ed. R. H. Campbell and A. S. Skinner (Indianapolis: Liberty Fund, 1981), p. 10.

171   Adam Smith, *Lectures On Jurisprudence*, ed. R. L. Meek, D. D. Raphael and P. G. Stein (Indianapolis: Liberty Fund, 1982), p. 567.

172   See Gordon Tullock, "The Welfare Costs of Tariffs, Monopolies, and Theft," *Western Economic Journal* 5, no. 3 (June 1967), pp. 224–32, and Anne Krueger, "The Political Economy of the Rent-Seeking Society," *American Economic Review 64*, no. 3 (June 1974), pp. 291–303.

173   For a detailed description of the most egregious example of the twentieth century, see Götz Aly, *Hitler's Beneficiaries: Plunder, Racial War, and the Nazi Welfare State*.

174   The origins and functioning of the apartheid system as such an example is explained by the classical liberal economist W. H. Hutt, *The Economics of the Colour Bar* (London: Andre Deutsch, 1964). White-dominated trade unions succeeded in imposing restrictions on the abilities of blacks to create wealth, thus eliminating them as competitors and reaping special rents (pp. 58–81). See also Ralph Horwitz, *The Political Economy of South Africa* (New York: Frederick A. Praeger Publishers, 1967).

175   Taming violence as a means to create incentives for savings, investment, and productivity is the theme of Robert H. Bates's *Prosperity and Violence: The Political Economy of Development* (New York: W. H. Norton, 2001).

176   For a treatment of the virtues of liberalism, see Deirdre N. McCloskey, *The Bourgeois Virtues: Ethics for an Age of Commerce* (Chicago: University of Chicago Press, 2006). See also Thomas

L. Haskell, "Capitalism and the Origins of the Humanitarian Sensibility," parts I and II, *American Historical Review 90*, no. 2 (April 1985), pp. 339–61 and no. 3 (June 1985), pp. 547–66.

177   "After 1795 many parishes in the South, following the policy of the magistrates of Speenhamland, began to give outdoor relief according to a scale based on the price of bread and the size of the family. There was nothing to object to in this: it was only sensible and humane to see that the income of the poor did not fall below the minimum of subsistence. But many of the authorities, confusing the problem of the wage-earner with that of the pauper, undertook to make up from the rates the amount by which the wages of the labourer fell short of their standard. A grant of relief that varies inversely with earnings is the worst form of subsidy, wince it destroys the incentive for the worker to demand, or employer to offer, higher wages." T. S. Ashton, *The Industrial Revolution*, p. 89.

178   Alexis de Tocqueville, *Memoir on Pauperism* (Chicago: Ivan R. Dec. 1997), p. 37.

179   Ibid., p. 58. Tocqueville clearly distinguished "voluntary charity" from "legal charity" and endorsed the former as establishing a "moral tie" "between those two classes whose interests and passions so often conspire to separate them from each other, and although divided by circumstances they are willingly reconciled. This is not the case with legal charity. The latter allows the alms to persist but removes its morality. The law strips the man of wealth of a part of his surplus without consulting him, and he sees the poor man only as a greedy stranger invited by the legislator to share his wealth." (p. 60)

180   Ibid., pp. 62–63.

181   See, for example, the treatment in Jason L. Riley, *Let Them In: The Case for Open Borders*, esp. 91–125. As Riley concludes, "If conservatives are worried about too many snouts at the trough—and if they're remotely interested in any sort of ideological consistency—they should be working to restrict welfare payments, not immigrants." (p. 125)

182   Benjamin M. Friedman, *The Moral Consequences of Economic Growth* (New York: Alfred A. Knopf, 2005), p. 39.

183   See, for example, Franz Oppenheimer, *The State* (Indianapolis: Bobbs-Merrill, 1914). "There are two fundamentally opposed means whereby man, requiring sustenance, is impelled to obtain

the necessary means for satisfying his desires. These are work and robbery, one's own labor and the forcible appropriation of the labor of others." (p. 24) Oppenheimer labeled the former the "economic means" and the latter the "political means." See also Vilfredo Pareto, *Sociological Writings*, ed. S. E. Finer (Totowa, NJ: Rowman and Littlefield, 1976), especially the discussions of "spoliation."

184 See, for example, Herbert Spencer, *Structure, Function and Evolution*, ed. Stanislav Andreski (New York: Charles Scribner's Sons, 1971), pp. 153–65.

185 See, in the context of state-imposed disadvantages on the basis of race, Walter Williams, *The State against the Blacks*.

186 Henry Summer Maine described "the movement of the progressive societies" from inherited relations, based on family membership, to personal liberty and civil society as "a movement from Status to contract." Henry Summer Maine, *Ancient Law* (New Brunswick, NJ: Transaction, 2003), p. 170.

187 E. L. Godkin, "The Eclipse of Liberalism," *The Nation*, August 9, 1900. He continued in a very pessimistic vein, "But it now seems that its material comfort has blinded the eyes of the present generation to the cause which made it possible. In the politics of the world, Liberalism is a declining, almost a defunct force."

188 See G. A. Cohen, "Incentives, Inequality, and Community," in *The Tanner Lectures on Human Values, vol. 13*, ed. B. Peterson (Salt Lake City: University of Utah Press, 1992), pp. 263–329, and Phillip Green, *The Pursuit of Inequality* (New York: Pantheon Books, 1981).

189 Jean-Baptiste Say, *A Treatise on Political Economy* (New York: Augustus M. Kelley, 1971), p. 133.

190 Ibid., 137. See also Jean-Baptiste Say, *Letters to Mr. Malthus* (London: Sherwood, Neely, and Jones, 1821), pp. 3–4: "Let us only look back two hundred years, and suppose that a trader had carried a rich cargo to the places where New York and Philadelphia now stand; could he have sold it? Let us suppose even, that he had succeeded in founding there an agricultural or manufacturing establishment; could he have there sold a single article of his produce? No, undoubtedly. He must have consumed them himself. Why do we now see the contrary? Why is the merchandize carried to, or made at Philadelphia or New York, sure to be sold at the current price? It seems to me

evident that is because the cultivators, the traders, and now even the manufacturers of New York, Philadelphia, and the adjacent provinces, create, or send there, some productions, by means of which they purchase what is brought to them from two other quarters." The implications for the classical liberal theory of international relations are obvious and seriously undercut the arguments of advocates of protectionism, as also of imperialist mercantilism.

191 Douglass C. North, "Institutions," *Journal of Economic Perspectives 5, no. I* (Winter 1991), p. 97. See also Douglass C. North, *Structure and Change in Economic History* (New York: W. W. Norton, 1981), pp. 201–2: "Institutions are a set of rules, compliance procedures, and moral and ethical behavioral norms designed to constrain the behavior of individuals in the interests of maximizing the wealth or utility of principles."

192 Daniel Shapiro, *Is the Welfare State Justified?* p. 5.

193 "The state can legislate a minimum wage rate. It can hardly require employers to hire at that minimum wage all those who were formerly employed at wages below the minimum." Milton Friedman, *Capitalism and Freedom* (Chicago: University of Chicago, 2002), p. 180.

194 Mancur Olson, *Power and Prosperity* (New York: Basic Books, 2000), pp. 111–34.

195 Vilfredo Pareto, *Sociological Writings*, p. 162.

196 For contemporary evidence, see W. Michael Cox and Richard Alm, *Myths of Rich and Poor* (New York: Basic Books, 1999), especially the discussion of upward mobility in incomes (pp. 69–78).

197 Ludwig Lachmann, "The Market Economy and the Distribution of Wealth," in Lachmann, *Capital, Expectations, and the Market Process* (Kansas City: Sheed Andrews and McMeel, 1977), p. 313.

198 Jean-Baptiste Say, *A Treatise on Political Economy*, p. 62.

199 Joyce Appleby notes, in her chapter on "The Dutch as a Source of Evidence," why the relatively "resource-poor" Dutch achieved enormous levels of per capita wealth: "The Dutch has been willing to nurture this complex social organization of the market by protecting the individual initiative on which it throve."

Economic Thought and Ideology in Seventeenth-Century England (Princeton, NJ: Princeton University Press, 1978), p. 96.

200   Adam Smith, *Essays on Philosophical Subjects*, p. 322.

201   Sarah Grimké, "Legal Disabilities of Women," in *Freedom, Feminism, and the State*, ed. Wendy McElroy (Oakland: Independent Institute, 1991), p. 107.

202   Bernard Bosanquet, "Institutions as Ethical Ideas," in *The Philosophical Theory of the State and Related Essays*, ed. Gerald F. Gaus and William Sweet (South Bend, IN: St. Augustine's Press, 2001), p. 280.

203   As the classical liberal Soviet dissident Vladimir Bukovsky pointed out in his memoirs, "Khrushchev wasn't very far from the truth when he said in one of his speeches: 'If people in our country would cease stealing for even a single day, communism could have been built long ago.' But the thing he failed to understand was that, without this stealing, the Soviet system wouldn't work at all. Without these rigged figures and manipulations hardly a single target would be met, and without this private, hence illegal, initiative, nothing at all would be produced in our country. All these collective and State farms that have become showplaces, without turnovers in the millions, wouldn't have survived for one minute if they hadn't been managed by swindlers." Vladimir Bukovsky, *To Build a Castle: My Life as a Dissenter* (London: Andre Deutsch, 1978), pp. 150–51.

204   Norman Barry, *Welfare* (Buckingham: Open University Press, 1990), p. 120.

205   Otto von Gierke, *Community in Historical Perspective*, ed. Antony Black (Cambridge: Cambridge University Press, 1990), p. 205. See also Antony Black, *Guild and State* (New Brunswick, NJ: Transaction, 2003), esp. pp. 167–83.

206   David Schmidtz, "Taking Responsibility," in David Schmidtz and Robert E. Goodin, *Social Welfare and Individual Responsibility*, p. 95.

207   David Beito, *From Mutual Aid to the Welfare State: Fraternal Societies and Social Services, 1890–1967*, p. 24.

208   David Green makes much of the involvement of the medical profession in promoting the National Insurance Act of 1911, which substituted a monopsony controlled by doctors and their

political allies for the competitive market created by multiple friendly societies of working people. See David Green, *Working Class Patients and the Medical Establishment*; the result of substituting involuntary taxes for voluntary dues as a source of payment was, as Green dryly notes, that "pay increases were far more easy to obtain than in the market." (p. 115). The other result was the waning of the friendly societies, as working people found themselves paying twice for the same access to medical services—once to a friendly society or affiliated medical institute, and again to the state.

209   David G. Green, *Reinventing Civil Society*, p. 46.

210   John Stuart Mill, "The Claims of Labour," in *The Collected Works of John Stuart Mill*, vol. 4: *Essays on Economics and Society*, part I, ed. John Robson (Toronto: University of Toronto Press, 1967), p. 372.

211   In Bernard Bosanquet's words, "Morality . . . consists in the social purpose working by its own force on the individual will. Economic Socialism is an arrangement for getting the social purpose carried out just not by its own force, but by the force of those compulsory motives or sanctions which are at the command of the public power." Bernard Bosanquet, "The Antithesis between Individualism and Socialism" (1890), in Bosanquet, *The Philosophical Theory of the State and Related Essays*, p. 329. See also Tibor R. Machan, *Generosity: Virtue in Civil Society* (Washington, DC: Cato Institute: 1998).

212   Adam Smith, *The Theory of Moral Sentiments* (Indianapolis: Liberty Fund, 1982), p. 178.

213   Ibid., p. 80.

214   Ibid.

215   See ibid, p. 163: "Without this sacred regard to general rules, there is no man whose conduct can be much depended upon."

216   Ibid., p. 138.

217   Bertrand De Jouvenel, *The Ethics of Redistribution*, p. 42.

218   Ibid., p. 44.

219   John Stuart Mill, "The Claims of Labour," p. 374.

220   Ibid. Bernard Bosanquet noted the unpromising history of state provision of welfare: "It is often alleged that the time of the factory development a hundred years ago was a time of unmixed Economic Individualism. But this is not so; perhaps the worst evils of that time arose directly from the intentionally lax or 'socialistic' Poor Law. It was the public institutions that for the most part supplied the children who were ill-treated." Bosanquet, "The Antithesis between Individualism and Socialism," p. 330.

221   See David Schmidtz's essay in Schmidtz and Goodin, *Social Welfare and Individual Responsibility*, especially the section on "Consequences Matter," pp. 86–88.

222   Wilhelm Röpke, *A Humane Economy: The Social Framework of the Free Market* (Indianapolis: Liberty Fund, 1971), p. 177.

223   Ibid., p. 175.

224   Milton Friedman, *Capitalism and Freedom*, p. 188.

225   Ibid., p. 191.

226   F. A. Hayek, *The Constitution of Liberty* (Chicago: University of Chicago Press, 1960), p. 257.

227   Nozick, *Anarchy, State, and Utopia*, p. 268.

228   A. V. Dicey, *Lectures on the Relation between Law and Public Opinion in England during the Nineteenth Century* (Indianapolis: Liberty Fund, 2008), p. 182.

229   Herbert Spencer, *The Man vs. the State*, in *Political Writings*.

230   See Sheri Berman, *The Primacy of Politics: Social Democracy and the Making of Europe's Twentieth Century*, on the common intellectual roots of Marxism, fascism, national socialism, and social democracy.

231   François Guizot, "Mémoires pour server à l'histoire de mon temps," in *Western Liberalism: A History in Documents from Locke to Croce*, ed. E. K. Bramstead and K. J. Melhuish (London: Longman Group, 1978), pp. 335–36.

232   Wilhelm von Humboldt, *The Limits of State Action* (Cambridge: Cambridge University Press, 1969), p. 40. See also the description of the opposition of German liberals to Bismarck's modern

welfare state in Ralph Raico, "Der Aufstieg des modernen Wohlfartsstaates und die liberale Antwort," in Raico, *Die Partei der Freiheit: Studien zur Geschichte des deutschen Liberalismus* (Stuggart: Lucius & Lucius, 1999), pp. 153–79.

233 Adam Smith, *The Theory of Moral Sentiments*, p. 82.

234 Compare Samuel Pufendorf on "connate" and "adventitious" obligations: "Now obligation can, by reason of its origin, be divided into connate and adventitious. The former belongs to all men immediately upon birth by virtue of the fact that they are such, fully exerting itself as soon as they have begun to be able, on account of their age, to understand its force and to regulate their action through reason . . . . Adventitious obligations are those voluntarily assumed by those who have already been born, or those enjoined by the command of a superior or by law." *The Political Writings of Samuel Pufendorf*, ed. Craig L. Carr, trans. Michael J. Seidler (Oxford: Oxford University Press, 1994), p. 50.

235 See, for example, the efforts by Anne Robert Jacques Turgot to eliminate forced peasant labor (the corvée) in France, described in *The Life and Writings of Turgot*, ed. W. Walker Stephens (New York: Burt Franklin, 1971), esp. pp. 124–49.

236 John Prince Smith, "On the Significance of Freedom of Trade in World Politics," in Bramstead and Melhuish, *Western Liberalism*, p. 357. The insistence on the value of unilateral free trade by classical liberals has received greater emphasis in recent years; see Razeen Sally, *Trade Policy, New Century: The WTO, FTAs, and Asia Rising* (London: Institute of Economic Affairs, 2008).

237 For recent works, see Philippe Legrain, *Immigrants: Your Country Needs Them* (London: Little, Brown, 2006), and Jason L. Riley, *Let Them In: The Case for Open Borders*.

238 The term "globalization" has many meanings. The project of the Soviet Union, for example, entailed worldwide imposition of one-party Communist rule; that is one kind of "globalization." Even nationalist and anticosmopolitan forces promote a kind of "globalization," in the form of a global movement of competing nationalisms, an idea that contains the seeds of endless conflict. Classical liberals have promoted certain universal standards of peaceful interaction through voluntary trade, tourism, travel, migration, and exchange of ideas. The result is compatible with a wide variety of different cultural forms, although

hostile to any that are imposed by force on nonconsenting parties. For classical liberal treatments of such topics, see Tom G. Palmer, *Globalization and Culture: Homogeneity, Diversity, Identity, Liberty* (Berlin: Liberales Institut, 2004), http://tomgpalmer.com/wp-content/uploads/papers/liberales2.pdf, and "Globalization, Cosmopolitanism, and Personal Identity," *Etica & Politica*, no. 2 (2003), http://tomgpalmer.com/wp-content/uploads/papers/palmer-globcosmoidentity.pdf. Classical liberals have been disparaged by socialist critics as "neoliberals," a term that virtually no classical liberal has accepted, partly because the term is used to refer not only to freer trade, travel, and migration but to often very illiberal statist development programs promoted by state-backed organizations, such as the World Bank, the International Monetary Fund, and the USAID, which classical liberals have traditionally opposed.

Index

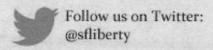

Students For Liberty provides resources for pro-liberty students and student groups, including:

- Student Conferences
- Leadership Handbooks and Training
- Free Books
- Tabling Kits
- Academic Webinar Series
- Academic Symposia

Find out more about our resources and **join the student movement for liberty** at:

www.studentsforliberty.org

Enroll Today! The Atlas Leadership Academy

The mission of the Atlas Economic Research Foundation, also known as the Atlas Network, is to discover, develop and support Intellectual Entrepreneurs worldwide who advance the Atlas vision of a society of free and responsible individuals. Atlas nurtures and collaborates with nearly 400 partners in the U.S. and over 80 countries.

Whether you're thinking of starting your own organization, are an associate at a think tank, a director of development or an executive director, the Atlas Leadership Academy (ALA) provides the opportunities you need to advance your beliefs in the free market. ALA is a flexible curriculum that allows you to gain the skills needed to succeed in the free market think tank world.

This program provides:

- Training on classical liberal values
- A six week course to help you determine how you can contribute to the cause of liberty
- Introductory and advanced think tank management courses (both online and live)
- Specialized online skills training

We know that your scarcest resource is your time, and these programs allow you to gain these skills on *your* schedule, when it's convenient and useful for you. Atlas caters to a worldwide network of free market leaders, and now, anyone can have access to our exciting products and training.

Enroll in the Atlas Leadership Academy today at AtlasNetwork.org/ALA.

"A superb introduction to the folly of the welfare state. The historical examples, the discussion of adverse consequences from existing welfare programs, and the moral arguments against government-imposed redistribution are all compelling background. Your future depends on understanding what is in this book."

—Jeffrey Miron, Director of Undergraduate Studies
in the Department of Economics at Harvard University

You Can Help Tell Young People About
After the Welfare State

Young people today are being robbed—of their rights, of their freedom, of their dignity, of their futures. This path-breaking book combines history, economics, philosophy, and public policy to diagnose the problem and prescribe solutions.

Please consider giving copies of this book to students and teachers, local political, business, and labor associations, the news media, and to your activist friends. Knowledge offers the power to change the future. This book will give you that power.

Special Bulk Copy Discount Schedule

1 book $ 8.95	25 books $ 95.00	500 books $1,250.00
5 books $25.00	50 books $175.00	1000 books $2,000.00
10 books $45.00	100 books $325.00	

All prices include postage and handling.

JAMESON BOOKS, INC   **ORDER TOLL FREE**
Post Office Box 738   **800-426-1357**
Ottawa, IL 61350

Please send me _____ copies of *After the Welfare State*.

Enclosed is my check for $ _____ or please charge my [ ] MasterCard   [ ] Visa

No._____ Exp. Date_____

Signature_____ Telephone_____

Name_____

Address_____

City_____ State_____ Zip_____

Illinois residents please add 6.5% sales tax. Please allow 2 weeks for delivery.

"A superb introduction to the folly of the welfare state. The historical examples, the discussion of adverse consequences from existing welfare programs, and the moral arguments against government-imposed redistribution are all compelling background. Your future depends on understanding what is in this book."

—Jeffrey Miron, Director of Undergraduate Studies
in the Department of Economics at Harvard University

You Can Help Tell Young People About
After the Welfare State

Young people today are being robbed—of their rights, of their freedom, of their dignity, of their futures. This path-breaking book combines history, economics, philosophy, and public policy to diagnose the problem and prescribe solutions.

Please consider giving copies of this book to students and teachers, local political, business, and labor associations, the news media, and to your activist friends. Knowledge offers the power to change the future. This book will give you that power.

Special Bulk Copy Discount Schedule

1 book $ 8.95	25 books $ 95.00	500 books $1,250.00
5 books $25.00	50 books $175.00	1000 books $2,000.00
10 books $45.00	100 books $325.00	

All prices include postage and handling.

JAMESON BOOKS, INC   **ORDER TOLL FREE**
Post Office Box 738   **800-426-1357**
Ottawa, IL 61350

Please send me _____ copies of *After the Welfare State*.

Enclosed is my check for $_____ or please charge my [ ] MasterCard [ ] Visa

No._____ Exp. Date_____

Signature_____ Telephone_____

Name_____

Address_____

City_____ State_____ Zip_____

Illinois residents please add 6.5% sales tax. Please allow 2 weeks for delivery.